UNDERSTANDING

BREEDING
MANAGEMENT

YOUR **GUIDE** TO HORSE HEALTH
CARE AND MANAGEMENT

ISBN 1-58150-018-1

Printed in the United States of America
First Edition: May 1999
1 2 3 4 5 6 7 8 9 10

UNDERSTANDING

BREEDING MANAGEMENT

YOUR **GUIDE** TO HORSE HEALTH CARE AND MANAGEMENT

By Christine M. Schweizer, DVM, Diplomate ACT
Foreword by Robert Hillman, DVM, MS, Diplomate ACT

The Blood-Horse, Inc. Lexington, KY

Contents

FOREWORD

The first International Symposium on Equine Reproduction held in 1974 at Cambridge, U.K. brought together the leading researchers in equine reproduction from all over the world. Discussions at this meeting served as a catalyst and stimulated a great increase in research studies on all phases of equine reproduction. While these studies are continuing at an increasingly sophisticated level, they have already produced a tremendous amount of new information that has permitted many improvements in broodmare management and therapeutic protocols. When properly used, the incorporation of this newer information has produced increased conception and foaling rates, which in turn resulted in a larger, healthier foal crop. However, much of this information has been published in diverse and fragmented sources.

In *Understanding Breeding Management* and in the companion text *Understanding the Broodmare*, Dr. Christine Schweizer has pulled this new information together and combined it with the wisdom of her considerable clinical experience. The result is a well-organized, easily followed text that is carefully indexed so that the reader can quickly locate an area of concern and extract the latest techniques to address the problem.

In *Understanding Breeding Management* the reproductive cycle of the mare, breeding management practices, and potential infertility problems are fully discussed. Throughout the texts, in addition to discussing therapeutic options to be used when problems occur, Dr. Schweizer emphasizes management procedures that can be employed to prevent these problems.

Dr. Schweizer has done an extraordinary job of bringing together a large volume of information and condensing and organizing it in a coherent and easily readable manner. The information in *Understanding Breeding Management* and *Understanding the Broodmare* is current and complete. These two books will be valuable assets to the seasoned broodmare manager seeking the newest techniques and therapies as well as a complete "how to" manual for the neophyte broodmare owner.

Robert Hillman, DVM, MS
Diplomate ACT
Senior Clinician Emeritus, NYSCVM
Cornell University

INTRODUCTION

My first lessons in the mare's estrous cycle came when I was approximately 11 years old and learning how to "walk hots" on the Belmont Park backstretch. I had known about "the birds and the bees" for some time (much to the dismay of my second grade teacher!), thanks to summers spent on a family farm in the Midwest and having had my pet cat, fish, and hamsters voluminously reproduce. But I had no real knowledge about the details of how mares behaved other than the obvious basics and romanticized versions from the horse stories I avidly read. Every now and again, as I would begin the 30 to 60 minute process of cooling out the racehorses after their morning workouts, a filly's groom would say to me, "Now be careful, Chrissy. This filly is 'horsing,' so don't let any colts get behind you."

I was a little mystified as to what exactly that meant, although I understood the sexual reference. (Did she just have a funny look in her eye that clued in the groom to her condition?) I had never actually observed a mare posturing and winking, and the illustrators of children's books usually did not depict this facet of equine behavior. I soon figured it out, however, as my experience increased and I discovered some non-fiction horse texts in the public library.

I eventually progressed to handling mares and stallions in

breeding situations, working on a breeding farm owned by the vet I worked for in high school, and later on at the university horse farm in college and veterinary school. It has become my daily work as a veterinarian.

Every mare is an individual, and every mare I have worked with has taught me something new about the sometimes subtle and not so subtle nuances and workings of the mare's reproductive cycle. The great fun of being a veterinarian and working with horses is that the learning never stops. There are always new observations to ingest and ruminate over. Successfully breeding mares sometimes can be very challenging, but it is never boring. It has been my experience that the more thorough, observant, and careful the breeding management of a mare is, the more likely the effort is to be rewarded with the eventual birth of a foal.

I have been very blessed to have the opportunity to spend my days doing exactly what I love doing most — working with horses and their owners. I would like to dedicate this text to all of my clients over the years who have honored me by trusting me with their dreams, and their wonderful mares, foals, and stallions who have taught me so much. I also would like to dedicate this text to Carol Collyer, farm manager at the Cornell Equine Research Park, and Liane Dillon, my technician and assistant in the Section of Theriogenology at Cornell University. Their dedication, knowledge, camaraderie, and horsemanship keep me moving all the long days of the breeding and foaling season, and their friendship is much enjoyed and cherished.

Endeavoring to breed a mare so that she produces a foal imparts a great responsibility on the mare owner. He or she is not only responsible for the health and welfare of the mare and her foal from conception to weaning and beyond, but the owner also bears the responsibility for the entire life of that foal he or she has caused to come into the world.

There are a great many horses. Will this new life have a secure place in our "throw away" society? The mare owner has a responsibility to this resulting young horse to ensure it is provided with a good start in life that will stand it in good stead all the days of its existence. Nutrition, health care, an environment that is safe and clean and affords plenty of room to exercise, handling, and a sound start to the foal's training (halter, lead rope, and manners) are all important. Likewise, genetics are important, too, and there is a responsibility to a breed's gene pool as well. A mare owner must be objective about a mare's qualities before making the decision to breed her. Does she have something important to contribute and pass on to her breed? Her pedigree, temperament, conformation, health, soundness, breed type, and athletic ability all must be carefully viewed and weighed in this decision. Not every uterus that is open should be filled. Just some food for thought.

During the course of writing *Understanding the Broodmare*, it soon became obvious it was going to require two texts to complete the telling of the mare's reproductive "saga," and I am very fortunate to have understanding and supportive editors at *The Blood-Horse* who have permitted me to do just that. In continuing on with *Understanding Breeding Management*, I have endeavored to address a few of the problems and questions I frequently encounter in a broodmare practice, and in so doing help mare owners have a better understanding of the mare's cycles, seasons, difficulties, and the breeding process as a whole. The goal here is to help the mare owner feel more comfortable with the process and be able to make informed decisions.

I hope the following pages contain information that will be useful to both the novice and the experienced broodmare owner. The knowledge offered within this book is not intended, however, to replace a veterinarian's "hands on" advice and expertise.

Breeding some mares sometimes can feel like trying to pound the proverbial square peg into a round hole. When something seems harder than it should be, there is usually a reason. This is an obvious red flag that a closer look at the mare's reproductive tract, the stallion, and/or the management is probably in order. Some mares have an obvious problem that hopefully can be remedied by treatment and/or more intensive management. Some mares just require patience and persistence. All mares benefit from a little luck.

There are few things more wonderful than watching a new life take hold and develop. It is always fun to be at an equine event and reflect that I knew a given horse when he or she was only a 2 centimeter embryo on my ultrasound screen. May your mares all be blessed with these little "black circles" in the breeding seasons to come.

Christine M. Schweizer, DVM,
Diplomate ACT
Cornell University
Ithaca, New York

CHAPTER 1

The Anatomy of a Broodmare

The broodmare is at once one of the most delightful and one of the most frustrating creatures a horse owner or veterinarian may encounter. The mare's reproductive cycle and behavior are such that even though a given mare usually follows the basic reproductive script of her species, she often will put her own individual spin on events. She might be perfectly normal; she just doesn't choose to be average. Mares will differ in intensity of behavioral signs of receptivity, reproductive tract changes, and size of ovarian follicles just before ovulation. To make matters worse, mares also will vary these findings depending on whether it is early or late in a breeding season. Fortunately, however, most mares are consistent in their "reproductive expression" on an individual basis and will tend to repeat behaviors and findings cycle to cycle. It is extremely important, therefore, to maintain accurate records and observe mares closely.

Mares' ovulations are notoriously difficult to predict exactly, and average pregnancy rates per cycle bred are in the neighborhood of 50-65%. Mares also experience a high percentage of early embryonic loss. It is therefore advantageous for mare managers to "stack the deck" in their favor to successfully breed a mare. This is especially true when assisted reproductive techniques such as artificial insemination with extended, chilled semen and frozen equine semen are being applied. Good management is vital to successful breeding of mares, and careful observation and accurate, complete records are necessary components of any breeding program.

ANATOMY OF THE MARE'S REPRODUCTIVE TRACT

The mare's reproductive tract is made up of internal and external structures. The mare has two kidney-shaped ovaries (a left one and a right one), each with a distinct ovulation fossa where the surface indents. All of a mare's ovulations (rupture of an ovarian follicle with simultaneous release of a fertilizable egg (or oocyte) occur through these fossae. The mare's oviducts (uterine tubes) attach at the site of the ovulation fossa and receive the ovulated oocyte. The oviducts are the site of fertilization and early embryonic development. Each oviduct connects to the uterus at the tip of each uterine horn, through a papilla. This papilla is called the tubo-uterine junction.

The equine uterus is shaped like a capital "T." The left and right uterine horns form the crossbar, and the uterine body forms the base. Where the base of each uterine horn meets the apex of the uterine body is called the "bifurcation." The uterine body ends at the mare's cervix. The role of the uterus is to help transport sperm to the site of fertilization, the oviducts, and to nourish and support the developing foal throughout the mare's pregnancy. The ovaries, oviducts, and uterus are suspended on either side within the mare's pelvis by the left and right broad ligaments. The broad ligaments therefore are supportive tissues to the reproductive tract. The ovarian and uterine blood-supplying vessels run through these ligaments.

The cervix serves as one of three barriers between the outside world and the uterine lumen. It is a straight, tubular structure, about the length and width of an average person's index finger. It is composed of an internal uterine opening (or "os"); a body; and an external, vaginal os. The cervix con-

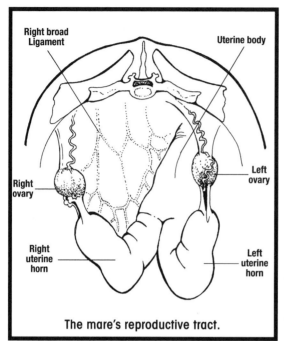

Right broad Ligament

Uterine body

Right ovary

Left ovary

Right uterine horn

Left uterine horn

The mare's reproductive tract.

nects the uterus to the vagina, and during pregnancy it is tightly closed, forming a barrier seal. During foaling the cervix must dilate fully so the foal can pass from the uterus into the birth canal.

The front (or cranial) end of the vagina begins at the external cervical os and the back of the vagina (or caudal vagina) ends at the vestibular-vaginal junction — the second barrier between the outside world and the uterine lumen. When fully extended, the equine vagina is about 12 inches long in the average 1,000 to 1,200-pound mare, and runs horizontally along the pelvic floor. The vagina has the dual role of being the copulatory organ and the birth canal. The vestibule connects the vagina to the vulva. The vestibular-vaginal junction forms a sphincter of tissue at about the level of the rear (or caudal) brim of the pelvis, and it is the location of the hymen when one is present. In a mare with good pelvic and perineal conformation, the vestibule slopes upward from the vulva to the vagina at about a 60° angle, and the vestibular-vaginal sphincter forms a tight seal between the vestibular and vaginal lumens. Just behind this sphincter, the urethra exits through the floor of the vestibule. The mare's clitoris also is in the floor of the vestibule just within the bottom commissure of the vulvar lips.

The mare's vulva is just below the anus and is made up of two labia, or lips. These lips form the third and final seal between the uterine lumen and the outside world. Mares with good perineal conformation have a vulva that is upright and in a straight vertical line with the anus. Two-thirds or more of the vulva should be below the floor of the pelvis, and the lips should meet evenly and tightly to effectively close the vulva. Any deviation so that the vulva is pulled above the floor of the pelvis and sloped forward predisposes the mare to aspirating air and fecal contamination into her vagina ("windsucking" or "pneumovagina"). Any growths (melanomas are especially common in the perineal tissues of gray mares) or injuries with resultant scarring that interferes with the lips of the vulva meeting properly also could predispose a mare to "windsucking."

CHAPTER 2

The Reproductive Cycle of the Mare

"To everything there is a season." — Ecclesiastes 3:1

The mare's reproductive, or estrous cycle is, on average, 21 days. A follicle is a fluid-filled structure on the mare's ovary that contains the oocyte. Mares develop waves of multiple follicles once or twice in a 21-day period. A cycling mare, therefore, almost always has one or more follicles present on her ovaries at any time during her cycle. As one cycle ends, and the mare prepares for the next ovulation, one or two follicles from the current follicular wave will mature and become dominant and ovulatory. Those follicles that do not go on to ovulate regress and eventually disappear. In general, follicular development on the ovary is stimulated by the release of follicle stimulating hormone (FSH) by the pituitary. The mare will develop and ovulate a mature follicle that is between 35 to 50 millimeters (mm) in diameter on average. The cells lining the follicle produce the steroid hormone estrogen, which is responsible for causing all the behavioral and tubular tract (uterus and cervix) changes we associate with a mare "in heat" (receptivity to a stallion; "open," soft cervix; soft, edematous uterus). The follicular phase, or estrus, typically lasts five to seven days and ends with an ovulation.

When a mare ovulates and the oocyte passes through the ovulation fossa and into the oviduct, the follicular fluid is lost and the follicle collapses. Rupture of the follicular membrane causes bleeding, and the ovulated follicle normally fills back up with blood and forms a corpus hemorrhagicum or CH, a structure that lasts about 24 hours. The cells that formerly lined the follicle begin to change (luteinize), multiply, and reorganize under the influence of a second pituitary hormone, luteinizing hormone (LH), to form a corpus luteum (CL). The initial rise in LH is also the "trigger" that stimulates ovulation in the first place.

> ## AT A GLANCE
>
> • A mare's reproductive cycle lasts about 21 days.
>
> • The behavior of mares in heat can include "winking," and frequent urination. Estrus mares also can act restless.
>
> • In the wild, the breeding season occurs during spring and summer in response to daylight.
>
> • Maiden mares, mares with foals by their side, and mares which have received anabolic steroids might fail to show estrus behavior.

As the cells of the former ovarian follicle luteinize, they stop producing estrogen and begin to produce another steroid hormone, progesterone. Progesterone causes the mare to become unreceptive to the stallion, tightens and closes the mare's cervix, and stimulates the uterus to provide an environment supportive to a developing embryo. The ovarian, primary CL is responsible for maintaining the early equine pregnancy, and it also prevents the development of another ovulatory follicle. It takes four to six days after ovulation for the CL to fully mature and produce high levels (more than 5 nanograms per milliliter) of progesterone. The period during which the CL is initially forming is called metestrus. The CL has a life span of about 14 days in the non-pregnant mare. This "luteal phase" that is dominated by progesterone is called diestrus. If a pregnancy is not present by 14 days after ovulation, the lining of the uterus, the endometrium, produces the hormone prostaglandin. Prostaglandin destroys (or lyses) the CL and terminates progesterone production, allowing a dominant follicle to form from the current wave of follicles. The period between the termination of the CL and clear development of a dominant, ovulatory follicle is called proestrus. Day 1 of the 21-day cycle is considered the first day after ovulation. The non-pregnant mare's next ovulation usually occurs 21 days later, and the cycle repeats itself.

The tubular portion of the mare's reproductive tract, the uterus and cervix, changes in response to the different ovarian steroid hormones. During estrus, estrogen is the dominant hormone. Under its influence, the uterus becomes soft and limp. The folds of the endometrial lining become filled with edema and become prominent on palpation and on ultrasound examination of the uterus. This endometrial edema is particularly pronounced during proestrus and early estrus, and it is markedly less pronounced in many mares on the day they will ovulate. The cervix also is highly responsive to the follicular estrogen from the dominant follicle(s). During estrus the cervix softens and becomes edematous. As the cervix softens, the lumen of the cervix becomes increasingly open. The stallion is thought to ejaculate through the open cervix, depositing his semen directly into the mare's uterus. The mucosa of the mare's vagina also pinkens because of the increased blood flow to the tract during estrus, and the walls are moist with clear, lubricating mucus. The vulva of many estrus mares will likewise soften and lengthen under the effects of estrogen. Overall, the mare in heat has a tract that is "open" and "inviting" to facilitate the deposition and transport of semen. When a mare is in diestrus, the opposite is true.

During diestrus, progesterone from the CL dominates. The role of progesterone is to safeguard and facilitate the development of an embryo, as evidenced by changes in the tubular tract. The uterus becomes toned and tubular, and there is no edema. Uterine tone is thought to be important for making contractions that move the embryo through the uterine lumen, a process thought to be critical to maternal recognition of pregnancy. The cervix becomes firm and tightly closed. The vagina becomes dry and pale, and the vulva becomes shortened and tight as compared to an estrus mare. Taken all together, the tract of the diestrus mare basically hangs a "do not disturb" sign and the cervix maintains a tight barrier to keep intruders out.

The mare's behavior also reflects her cyclic changes. Under the influence of estrogen, she becomes increasingly receptive to a stallion's romantic overtures. When presented to a stallion she will stand still, move her tail to the side, urinate and/or flash her clitoris in and out of her vulva ("winking"), squat and posture with her hind end, and allow the stallion to mount and penetrate her vulva. Estrus mares' squatting, winking, and urinating frequently is sometimes referred to as "horsing."

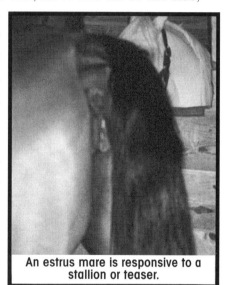

An estrus mare is responsive to a stallion or teaser.

Mares typically become restless during estrus and may walk the fence line, whinny and call to other horses, trying to seek out a mate. Many mares will stand as close as their stall or fence will allow to a stallion that might be as far away as another barn or paddock, and posture and try to get his attention. If there are no stallions around, a mare might tease to a gelding or mare, or even to a person. Early on in proestrus and early estrus the mare could demonstrate "lukewarm" receptivity, but the intensity of the signs usually increases so that the mare is "red hot" receptive within one to three days of her ovulation and could remain receptive 24 to 48 hours after ovulation. In general, mares are most receptive during the 24 hours surrounding ovulation. These shifts in intensity can be subtle, and it is important to pay attention to what the mare is saying. Most mares will demonstrate signs of heat for five to seven days, although some show signs for shorter or longer periods. It is therefore difficult to predict by behavior alone when a mare will ovulate. Retrospectively, ovulation can be assumed to have occurred 24 to 48 hours before the mare began "teasing out."

Under the influence of progesterone, the mare is motivated to reject a stallion's advances. This makes sense because an established pregnancy would be jeopardized and likely aborted if a pregnant mare were bred by a stallion (or inseminator!). If approached by a stallion, the mare's body language usually conveys her lack of enthusiasm for his propositioning, and frequently the "No!" will be violently enforced should the stallion persist. The mare will refuse to stand still, swish her tail, pin her ears, and possibly squeal and kick at the stallion. It is little wonder that stallions experienced at pasture breeding usually approach mares with caution. Some mares are not as vehement in their response as others (i.e., their idea of saying "No" could be just not saying "Yes"), but even those mares which stand quietly for the teaser during diestrus usually will refuse to allow themselves to be mounted. Mares will remain unreceptive until their next estrus period. That means it will be 14 to 18 days after an ovulation before an open mare begins showing signs of heat — i.e., once the progesterone from the lysed CL is gone from her system and estrogen released from the new ovulatory follicle is rising.

SEASONALITY OF THE EQUINE REPRODUCTIVE CYCLE

Mares are seasonally polyestrous, long day breeders. In simple terms, this means mares have multiple, repeating 21-day estrous cycles in response to increasing day length, and therefore have a well-defined breeding season that is limited to the spring and summer. In the northern hemisphere, mares in general will naturally cycle from March or April through

September or October. The peak of the equine breeding season is in May, June, and July. The winter months — November, December, January, and February — are marked by a period of anestrus (inactivity of the mare's ovaries and tract). Between the cycling and non-cycling periods are the spring and fall transitional periods.

The winter anestrus period is marked by a deep quiescence of the mare's ovaries and reproductive tract that mirrors the sleeping, snow-filled landscape around her. The ovaries become shrunken and small with little to no

Winter is an anestrous period for mares.

follicular activity. There is no progesterone and little if any estrogen in her system, and so the mare's uterus becomes thin, slack, and atonic with no signs of edema. The uterus of the anestrus mare is, therefore, often a challenge to palpate. The cervix likewise becomes inactive and, though it has palpable tone, it will vary from closed to mildly open. The appearance of the cervix, in contrast to the estrus cervix, will be pale and non-edematous. Anestrus mares frequently will be indifferent to a teaser and might even permit themselves to be mounted. There is no progesterone to tell them "No," but there is no estrogen to tell them "Yes" either, so they might be merely passive.

In the northern hemisphere, the shortest day of the year is the winter solstice, December 21. From this day through the next calendar year, the day length gradually increases. The increasing photoperiod stimulates the mare's pituitary gland (via the pineal gland and hypothalamus) to begin producing FSH, which in turn begins to stimulate the development of ovarian follicular activity. This "spring transition" from anestrus to normal cyclic activity is marked by the development of numerous large follicles that rise up and regress without ovulating in a repeated, overlapping fashion. Typically, during this period, mares will demonstrate irregular and/or prolonged heat periods under the influence of all this follicular activity. (I observed one mare who displayed continuous behavioral estrus for six straight weeks during one spring transitional period.) Eventually the mare recruits an ovulatory follicle, and the transitional period ends with the first ovulation of the spring. Many mares accomplish this first ovulation by or shortly after the spring equinox, March 21. After this first ovulation, the normal mare falls into her 21-day cyclic pattern for the remainder of the physiological breeding season, or until she becomes pregnant.

The normal events of the mare's estrous cycle have already been discussed; however, some generalized detailing of the patterns observed during the physiological breeding season are worth mentioning. In general, the initial heat periods during the early part of the spring tend to be longer (i.e., seven to nine days) and the mares tend to ovulate larger follicles (i.e., 50 to 60 mm follicles in the average Thoroughbred or warmblood mare) than they do later in the season. By May, June, and July, heat periods are usually five to seven days

The peak breeding season is in late spring and early summer.

long and mares are ovulating 40 to 50 mm follicles on average. The tendency for multiple ovulations during a single heat period also increases as the season progresses. Toward the end of the breeding season, heat periods can become abbreviated (i.e., three days or so), and mares sometimes begin to ovulate "small" (30 to 35 mm) follicles.

The longest day of the year is the summer solstice, June 21. After that the day length begins to decrease, and by the time the fall equinox has been reached on September 21, some mares are entering fall transition in preparation for shutting down for the winter. Fall transition is marked by the development of one to three large follicles during the final heat period of the season that "hang" and fail to go on to ovulate. Often these follicles become hemorrhagic after reaching peak diameter and staying that size for a couple of days (a change that is readily identifiable on ultrasound examination). These follicles do not luteinize, but rather gradually regress and disappear as the tract settles into anestrus. Occasionally mares will repeatedly bring up one or more additional anovulatory follicles and heat periods might appear prolonged or irregular before they settle down for the winter. By late October to early November, the majority of mares have entered fall transition, and by December most of them are in anestrus. A small percentage of mares appear to continue to cycle throughout the winter.

CYCLIC ABNORMALITIES

Mares which fail to show behavioral estrus during the physiological breeding season require investigation. They might be pregnant. Many mares presented to a veterinarian for infertility are found to be pregnant on rectal palpation and ultrasound examination. Any mare with an unknown or uncertain breeding history, who has had known or potential exposure to a stallion (even a yearling colt!), and who fails to behaviorally cycle, should be closely examined by a veterinarian before more invasive diagnostic procedures that would disrupt an existing pregnancy (i.e., uterine culture, cytology, or biopsy) are performed. Some mares cycle normally, but fail to give any outward indication of their heats. Maiden mares (mares which have never been bred), protective mares with foals at their sides, or mares which have received anabolic steroids commonly fail to show behavioral estrus when presented to a teaser even though they are cycling normally and are in heat (i.e., have a breedable, ovulatory follicle and no CL). Observe these mares carefully to pick up on subtle changes in behavior and external signs.

Maidens sometimes fail to show heat to a teaser because they are fearful and uncertain of the situation. These mares often will show heat to other mares, however, and if they are handled with care and patience and are not allowed to have a bad experience, they usually will start teasing well to a stallion after one or two cycles.

Mares with foals at their sides (especially foal heat mares) are

A twitch can get a mare's attention.

often more interested in protecting their babies from the teaser than demonstrating what their estrogen is telling them. These mares will frequently lift their tails, urinate, "wink," and "break down" into a still, squatting stance in their stalls, however, if they hear the sounds of a stallion teasing another mare at a perceived safe distance away. It behooves the mare manager to have someone stand and watch such mares in their stalls. Presenting the mare to the teaser away from her foal or with the foal safely restrained within her line of vision but away from the stallion sometimes works, and in some cases careful application of a twitch to restrain the mare will turn her attention to the sexual business at hand.

Performance mares which have been exposed to anabolic

steroids also will sometimes be cycling normally, but will not be receptive to teasing. These mares need time to allow the effects of the steroids to wear off (sometimes they never do), before they will demonstrate normal estrus behavior. It is ideal to turn out mares coming from a training/competition situation (once they have settled in), and allow them several months to unwind and become accustomed to the daily rhythms, sites, and sounds of stud farm life before being thrown into the hustle of the breeding season.

Mares which cycle normally but fail to demonstrate it behaviorally can be successfully bred, but they require more intensive breeding management and veterinary monitoring (i.e., daily rectal palpation and ultrasound, vaginal speculum examinations, etc.) to identify and monitor their estrus periods. In breeds which permit it, artificial insemination might be the only way to safely achieve a breeding with mares which violently resist being live covered by a stallion.

Very old mares which fail to show heat might truly be no longer cycling. There is reported evidence of mares older than 25 which experience reproductive senescence (menopause) much the same as women do. Our ability to effectively care for equine senior citizens through better diets and health care has led to an increase in the geriatric equine population in the past few years, and I think the number of observed "menopausal" mares will continue to grow.

Mares with abnormal chromosomal numbers usually fail to cycle altogether. Because their genetic programming has gone astray, ovarian function is absent or abnormal, and their reproductive organs are frequently atrophied. These mares might demonstrate a variety of behaviors and a variety of abnormalities in their reproductive tracts. The most common genetic abnormality is the presence of only a single X chromosome so that their karyotype is XO rather than XX. These mares are identical to women who have Turner's Syndrome. These mares are typically very passive (and will sometimes even allow themselves to be bred by a stallion much as occasional anestrous mares will do), but they usually do not demonstrate overt estrus signs.

Variations from the 21-day estrous cycle length also are observed frequently in mares during the normal spring/summer breeding season. Increased number of days between ovulations (increased interestrus interval) and decreased number of days between ovulations (short cycling) occur as a result in the prolongation or abbreviation, respectively, of the life span of the mare's CL (i.e., the diestrus period).

Prolonged diestrus (or "pseudopregnancy") in the horse is defined as maintenance of the CL beyond 15 days after ovulation in a non-pregnant mare. Retention of a CL might occur in as many as 15% to 20% of all estrous cycles, but the reasons remain sketchy.

Occasionally a mare will experience a prolonged diestrus period because she has a second ovulation during her diestrus period in spite of the negative feedback on the pituitary LH by progesterone from the already existent CL. This second CL is too young (less than six days old) to respond and be lysed by uterine prostaglandin when prostaglandin is produced by the uterine endometrium 14 days after the first ovulation. There is an overlap in progesterone production from the two waxing and waning CLs, so the mare remains in diestrus, and the second CL is retained. Early embryonic loss after maternal recognition of pregnancy also could result in retention of a CL. Uterine production of prostaglandin is blocked by the presence of the pregnancy so the CL is maintained, and the CL then persists after the embryo is lost. Mares which have extreme endometrial damage (usually from longstanding or severe infections, or from exposure of the uterine lining to harsh substances) might no longer be able to produce prostaglandin in sufficient quantities to effectively lyse a CL and will therefore retain a CL following an ovulation. These mares are particularly at risk of developing a pyometra (a dilated, fluid- and pus-filled uterus with a closed cervix and possibly an active CL on an ovary) if there are any organisms or established infections in the uterus at the time of ovulation. There also are many mares which retain their CL on any given cycle with no ready explanation as to why.

Prolonged diestrus in an open mare is readily treated by lysing the offending CL with a shot of prostaglandin administered by a veterinarian after careful examination to ensure that she is not pregnant. It is important to identify this condition as early as possible not only because of the risk of established uterine infections in some mares, but also because the retained CL can persist for as many as 60 days if left untreated, and valuable time during the limited breeding season can be lost waiting for such a mare to return to estrus on her own.

Mares which short cycle are the opposite of pseudopregnant mares. They have a premature release of prostaglandin from their endometrium (i.e., fewer than 14 days after ovulation), and therefore a shortened diestrus period. The mare's endometrium prematurely produces the prostaglandin most commonly in response to uterine irritation and inflammation (endometritis). The most common cause of endometritis is uterine infection, but it also might be incited by chronic endometrial exposure to urine (vaginal urine poolers) or air ("windsuckers"), or the presence of a foreign body. During estrus the mare's uterine defense systems are more active (i.e., uterine clearance of accumulated fluid and cells is heightened; the cervix is open so uterine drainage can occur; white blood cell defenses are more active; progesterone during diestrus suppresses neutrophil [WBC] function, etc.), and so an early return to estrus, or short cycling, can be viewed as nature's way of helping a mare help herself clear a uterine infection. Mares which have a history of short cycling need to be examined closely to determine the source of inflammation. Occasionally a mare will short cycle for no discernible reason, but this is the exception.

Ovarian tumors

The most commonly encountered ovarian tumor in the

mare, the granulosa-theca cell tumor (GCT), also will cause behavioral and apparent cyclic abnormalities in an affected mare. The GCT is a biologically active tumor that produces varying amounts of all the hormones normally produced by the cells lining the ovarian follicle, the granulosa and theca cells. Hormones produced include estrogen, progesterone, testosterone, and inhibin. Inhibin is a protein hormone produced by the ovulatory follicle that negatively feeds back on the pituitary to decrease FSH production. Mares might outwardly exhibit behavioral signs of prolonged estrus (nymphomania) or intermittent estrus, anestrus, or stallion-like behavior depending on the amount and ratio of the steroid hormones being produced by the ovarian tumor.

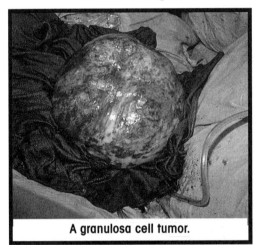

A granulosa cell tumor.

When palpated by a veterinarian during a rectal examination, the GCT usually presents as an enlarged ovary that has no discernible ovulation fossa. The opposite ovary usually will be small and quiescent (hormone production by the GCT suppresses pituitary stimulation of the ovaries, so the unaffected side is usually in an effective "anestrus" state). Rarely does the mare continue to cycle normally off of the unaffected ovary once a GCT has formed. On ultrasound examination the tumor will classically have a multi-follicular/cystic appearance with many small and/or large follicular structures. The unaffected ovary will be small and devoid of significant active structures (i.e., no follicles or CLs).

Diagnosis is made based on the mare's clinical signs and the classical findings of an enlarged "cystic" ovary on one side and an inactive ovary on the other. Occasionally it will be difficult to definitively assess by physical exam findings alone whether a GCT is the source of the problem (these tumors could start out small and in the early stages the opposite ovary might still be cycling normally), and hormonal assays might help to definitively diagnose the problem. Elevated testosterone and inhibin levels are considered to be diagnostic for GCT (although the lack of elevated levels of these two hormones does not rule out the problem). In cases where it is unclear, time usually will tell as these tumors tend to grow and can become quite large.

Fortunately they are usually slow to metastasize, although that has been reported to occur. GCTs have been reported in young and old mares alike as well as in pregnant and non-pregnant mares. Treatment is the surgical removal of the affected ovary. The non-affected ovary should recover and begin to cycle normally again within 12 months after the surgery. (The longer the GCT has been active, the longer it takes to recover function on the remaining ovary. Also, if surgery is performed in September, the mare could wait until the following breeding season to begin cycling again.) GCTs usually affect only one ovary but can occur in both or recur later in the originally unaffected ovary.

CHAPTER 3

Pre-Breeding Management

It is of paramount importance that any mare intended for breeding be in optimal health before the beginning of the breeding season. A Coggins test and annual vaccinations for Eastern and Western encephalitis, tetanus, rabies, and Potomac horse fever should all be updated before breeding. It is probably a good idea to give the mare a booster against rhinopneumonitis and influenza, too.

If the mare is going to be bred to a stallion positive for equine viral arteritis (EVA) and the mare does not have a protective titer against the disease, she also will require an EVA vaccination before being exposed to that stallion's semen. Owners of mares being bred with frozen semen also might wish to vaccinate previously unexposed mares for EVA as a precaution.

Prior to the breeding season, fecal examinations should be performed, and any parasite infestations corrected under a veterinarian's supervision. Ideally, mares already on a regular deworming schedule using anthelmintics should have their treatment coordinated with the first breeding cycle so that anthelmintics (even those considered safe for administration during pregnancy) will not be required during the first 60 days of pregnancy.

The mare's feet should be trimmed and cared for on a

regular basis as prescribed by a farrier and veterinarian. A potential broodmare's feet and legs need to be carefully evaluated before breeding to determine whether she can support the added weight of pregnancy without undue pain or stress. Likewise, if the mare has a chronic medical condition such as laminitis, Cushing's, or heaves, a critical and honest evaluation must be made as to whether the mare is capable of carrying a pregnancy to term and whether it is fair to ask her to try.

> ## AT A GLANCE
>
> • Mares should be current on vaccinations before being bred.
>
> • Mares being bred to EVA-positive stallions need to be vaccinated.
>
> • Regular deworming and foot care are important.
>
> • Age and physical condition should be considered.
>
> • Health and reproductive records should be maintained.

Dental maintenance also should be addressed before the breeding season. A veterinarian who is knowledgeable about equine dentistry should perform a thorough examination and correct any problems and perform the annual floating so that the mare can make the most of her diet and not have to undergo the stress of dental procedures during pregnancy.

The mare's overall body condition should be evaluated to ensure that she is neither too thin nor too overweight when it is time to breed her because both conditions sometimes hamper a mare's ability to settle. In addition, her coat and eyes should have a bright, healthy appearance and expression.

A potential broodmare's age also needs to be considered carefully. The optimum period of fertility for a mare seems to be between the ages of 6 and 11, and, correspondingly, foal birth weights also appear to be optimal when a mare is between 7 and 11 years of age. That is not to say an older mare cannot successfully conceive, carry her pregnancy to term, foal a healthy foal successfully, and raise that foal to be in a good, healthy, and appropriately grown condition at weaning. Many older mares do this just fine. In general, however, a mare's overall fertility decreases after she is 12 years old while her risk of pregnancy-related complications also increases. In general, the older girls will require especially careful management both at home and in the breeding shed to reproduce successfully. When considering a young mare (less than 4 to 6 years of age) for breeding, it is prudent to choose one which is physically mature enough to handle the demands of pregnancy and lactation without compromising her own or her potential foal's well-being, and to feed her appropriately to meet both her growth and pregnancy needs.

Many performance mares need time to "unwind."

Lastly, a comment on mares which are in athletic training or have recently retired. In my experience, a mare performs her best reproductively when she is allowed time to settle into the reproductive rhythms of her body and to become comfortable in her environment. Many athletic mares need time to unwind from their peak training condition, undergo "withdrawal" from anabolic steroids they might have received, and get re-accustomed to being out with other mares and competing in a "herd" situation before they will become pregnant and stay that way. With some mares, this can take months.

In an ideal universe the decision about whether to breed a performance mare is reached the fall before the breeding season. This way, the mare can take the fall and winter off to begin making these adjustments, and she can be teased and managed in the beginning of the breeding season (as opposed to the frantic and hectic middle and end months). This allows the extra time, patience, and handling a maiden mare will require while she is learning and adjusting to her new role in life. Events, however, don't always turn out as planned, and whether due to injury, lackluster performance, opportunity, or human capriciousness, mares often are asked to change from a performer to a broodmare literally overnight. It will require diligent management and observation for them to be bred successfully in a timely fashion. For some mares, no matter how well they are managed, time and persistence ultimately will be required.

A number of clinicians have noted that some mares recently out of training have the best chance of conceiving if bred on their very first estrus upon arrival from the training center (some as they literally come off the van!). If this first estrus and ovulation after training are missed, it usually takes the mares valuable time before they "get into the swing of things" and cycle and breed appropriately.

RECORD-KEEPING

The importance of accurate, detailed health and reproductive records when breeding and foaling mares cannot be overemphasized. The human memory is unreliable. Good record-keeping is vital to successful broodmare (and stallion!) management. Breeding records come in a variety of formats and technologies ranging from a well-marked wall calendar and individual mare cards in a notebook to elaborate computer systems. It makes little difference what system is used, provided that the system contains all the information required, recorded in a clear fashion. Information needs to be readily accessible and retrievable. Records by nature are useless if they are not well maintained, and the more complicated, time consuming, and inaccessible the system is, the less likely it is to be maintained.

Each mare needs to have a running health record that details her vaccinations, deworming schedule, hoof maintenance, dental maintenance, chronic medications, and any health problems (what they are/were, when they occurred, diagnostics performed, treatments administered, and outcomes). Notes that also mention and detail an individual mare's preferences, sensitivities, stable vices, and social skills also can be useful, especially if more than one person routinely cares for the horse or if the regular caretaker is unavailable for any reason.

Specific reproductive records for a given mare should be maintained season to season because mares tend to repeat breeding and foaling patterns. Initiate a record for each mare at the start of each season. Record such general information as the year, the mare's registered name, her age, owner, owner's address and telephone numbers, and previous pertinent reproductive history. The latter would include number of foals, foaling complications, breeding injuries, tendency to urine pool, previous abortions and their identified cause if known, and previous uterine biopsy scores.

Also record her status at the beginning of the current breeding season: maiden, open, barren, or foaling. A maiden mare is a non-pregnant mare which has never been bred. An open mare is a non-pregnant mare which previously has produced a foal but was not bred during the previous breeding season. A barren mare is a non-pregnant mare which was bred during the previous breeding season and either failed to establish a pregnancy or lost the pregnancy at some point during the gestation either through embryonic resorption or fetal abortion. A foaling mare is a pregnant mare which will foal sometime during the upcoming breeding season.

It is important to record a mare's status as it reflects possible management differences a given mare might require during the upcoming breeding season. For example, unless the mare is old or has a history of a certain problem, it is not anticipated that an "open mare" will be difficult to breed. On the other hand, a barren mare might require investigative work and a breeding soundness examination as well as more intensive monitoring and minimal contamination breeding techniques. A maiden mare, meanwhile, might require more time for patient handling.

To complete the "general" portion of an individual mare's reproductive record for a given breeding season, report the following: the name of the stallion to which she will be bred, his owner/manager, the address and phone number, whether the breeding is to be via natural cover or artificial insemination (fresh, extended cooled and shipped, or frozen), the stallion's collection or cover schedules, and availability of semen transport (same day air or overnight express).

Detailed records of each estrous cycle during the season a mare is monitored and/or bred are critical for effective management, and these records commence with the first reproductive-related event of that particular mare's season. For all non-pregnant mares it could begin as innocently as recording the date in November or December that the mares are put under lights and subsequent daily teasing activity leading up to and through the spring transitional period. (Mares typically will be up and cycling 60 to 90 days after the initiation of the artificially extended daily photoperiod).

For foaling mares, make daily notations on pre-foaling changes in her mammary gland and teat development, relaxation and softening of tail head and croup tissues, behavioral changes, and milk electrolyte values. Also report the date she foaled, the difficulty of the delivery, and any post-foaling complications, as well as the details of her first postpartum reproductive examination seven days after foaling and the progress of the foal heat.

For cycling mares, records of daily events should include how the mare teased and the findings of any veterinary examinations. Detailed information about ovarian structures, uterine and cervical tone, and the presence or absence of uterine fluid, edema, or an embryo should be noted. Other diagnostic findings such as uterine culture and cytology results along with any treatments should be recorded. Breedings should also be detailed and noted.

A variety of scoring and symbol systems are used to describe and categorize things such as type and quality of ovarian structures, uterine tone, and teasing intensity. Each one can be as individual as the people using it.

CHAPTER 4

Teasing

In the natural state, a stallion and mare interact continuously. This interaction allows the stallion to identify easily (by behavior, scent, persistence) when a mare is ready to permit breeding, and he follows through accordingly. The intensity of a mare's receptivity is linked closely to her ovulation. As a result, the fertility of wild horses is typically higher on a per-cycle basis than that of domestic mares. In most domestic management systems, mares and stallions are kept separate from one another until the actual moment of breeding and so it becomes the responsibility of the humans to determine when the mare is optimally ready to be bred. Teasing mares on a routine basis provides invaluable information about the mare's current cycle status and helps us determine how close the estrus mare might be to ovulating. Teasing is an important and highly recommended breeding management tool which should not be overlooked or disregarded unless a farm cannot accommodate the maintenance and handling of a teaser male.

The teaser is an integral part of any breeding management team. His job description, if printed, likely would read, "must be courtly, and a good conversationalist, attentive and tractable, sexy and persistent, but always a gentleman." A teaser can be either a stallion or a gelding which demonstrates good libido (many geldings still have plenty of will!). He needs to be talkative, but not a screamer who might unduly frighten a shy mare. He must be persistent and stimulatory to a mare. He should nuzzle, sniff, nudge, and nip at the mare but never be vicious or savage. It is equally important that he be easy to handle and obedient so that he will back away from a mare when directed to do so. It is also helpful if he has a good measure of sense and self-preservation to help him when he encounters mares which would just as soon kill him as

AT A GLANCE

- The intensity of a mare's response to a stallion or teaser is linked closely to her ovulation.

- Teasing is an important part of breeding management and should be part of a farm's daily routine.

- There are various ways to tease, including presenting an individual mare to a teaser in a controlled setting.

look at him. A teaser can be any breed or size, although some mare managers prefer to work with pony stallions. A teaser should be free of communicable diseases, have a negative Coggins, be up to date on his vaccinations, and receive regular health and maintenance care just like any other horse. A good teaser is worth his weight in gold and more than earns his oats and keep on any breeding farm.

Equally vital to a successful teasing program is a highly observant individual who can accurately interpret the behavioral interactions and displays of the teaser and the mare being teased. It is important that the same person observe the daily teasing sessions of each mare on the farm so that subtle nuances and shifts in a mare's behavior as she progresses through her cycle are more likely to be noticed. This individual may be the farm manager or another member of the farm personnel. The "tease man" must be exquisitely in tune with the reproductive behaviors of mares, and he or she must "know" each and every mare's individual behavior patterns well enough to interpret correctly what she is saying. As previously mentioned, the maintenance of complete and

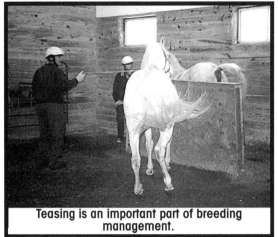

Teasing is an important part of breeding management.

accurate records is vital. Some mares are obvious in their behavior. They are blatantly "in" from the first day they are in estrus. They stand, break down and urinate, and wink the instant they come into contact with the teaser, and literally have to be pulled away from him when the session is completed. And they are blatantly "out" when they are in diestrus, such that they immediately pin their ears, swish there tails, move about at the first nicker of the teaser, and begin letting fly with their hind legs if the teaser so much as breathes on them. These mares can be like clockwork, teasing in for five to seven days and then teasing "out" for 16 to 18 days. These mares make it all look easy. Then you have the shy mares which routinely resist a stallion's advances even when they are approaching ovulation, but finally break down with a little patience and persistence on the part of the handlers and teasers. This mare's gradual receptivity could subtly intensify on the day of ovulation but not so much that the average observer off the street might notice. The extreme is the mare whose idea of receptivity is striking out with her front and rear feet, then perhaps standing still for a moment or two while the teaser cautiously sniffs her over. She routinely will submit only to this minor extent on the day she is ovulating.

Good records and having someone who can read each mare accurately are the only way of identifying behavioral estrus in these more difficult mares. The information and interpretation that an experienced and knowledgeable "tease man" provides to an examining veterinarian are invaluable in helping that veterinarian identify where a given mare might be in her overall cycle on a particular day, predicting how close she is to ovulation, and determining the best time to breed her.

There are various ways of teasing mares. One method is placing a teaser in a small fenced paddock in the middle of a larger pasture containing a group of mares, then watching to see which mares come visiting. One problem with this system is that a dominant mare in estrus may not permit a subordinate estrus mare to approach the teaser, and you run the risk of missing the submissive mares. There also is the problem of accurately identifying mares from a distance as well as having to sit on the fence all day watching (a pleasant way to occupy one's day, perhaps, but too inefficient for many management situations). Therefore, many farms prefer to present mares individually to the teaser in a controlled situation. This could take the form of placing the teaser and mare in large adjacent box stalls divided by a solid half wall and sliding window divider that can be opened so the two can interact freely with the half wall between them.

Another approach involves placing the stallion in a "tease box" where he is loose and free to extend his head and neck over a half wall to touch and sniff mares led up to him individually. Conversely, the teaser may be led to a mare's individual stall, where the two can interact through the doorway either by backing the mare part way out for the stallion to examine her hindquarters (brave teaser!) or by merely letting the stallion talk to the mare from outside the stall or over a closed dutch door. Finally, the mare and the teaser can be led individually to opposite sides of a tease wall where they can interact while remaining "in hand." No matter what system is used, safety for both the horses and the handlers should be a paramount consideration.

Sex is exciting. The teaser and the mare both will get a little wound up by this experience, and even when a mare is in "red hot standing heat" she can squeal and strike out at the stallion to convey to him that he should mind his manners.

Likewise, the teaser can strike out in retaliation or anxiety. Mares which are not in estrus are prone to displaying their displeasure by kicking out with their hind feet. For this reason, it is highly recommended to have a solid padded or wooden wall between the horses to ensure their safety. (There is also the added benefit of having a barricade of sorts between the teaser and the mare just in case the teaser stallion decides he would like to be the main performer for a change and not just the warm-up act.)

While it might be tempting to tease over already existing fences or gaits, it is not a good idea because it is easy for one of the horses to entangle a leg should it kick or strike out. Likewise, it is not safe for the teaser to have to approach the hind end of a mare which has been backed through her stall door. I have observed one valiant pony teaser launched across the shed row by a mare with exceedingly good aim. Fortunately for the pony he was not seriously injured; he picked himself up, gave a good shake, then came back for more. I once had to euthanize a different pony teaser who was not so lucky and received fractured ribs and a punctured lung for his enthusiasm.

Handlers need to be calm, professional, observant, and cautious. When horses are being teased in hand, the handler needs to be in control without interfering, and at the same time remain out of harm's way. The handler should never allow himself to be directly in front of or behind either horse, or caught between the two horses. Probably the best place to stand to be relatively safe from both teeth and hooves and retain control is off to the left side at the level of the horse's shoulder. The handler should hold the shank so that each horse remains under control but has some freedom to interact. Too much slackness in the lead raises the risk of the handler or the horses becoming entangled.

In my opinion anyone who undertakes the responsibility of handling a mare or stallion in a teasing or breeding situation needs to be the consummate horseman and well experienced handling horses in all types of frightening situations. The breeding shed is no place for egos and bravado. It is extremely important for everyone's safety (man and beast) that handlers in these situations be well trained and competent. Novices just becoming initiated to the equine breeding routines and activities need to learn under the tutelage of an experienced horseman. Too much can go wrong too quickly and with dire consequences.

Teasing mares should be part of the daily routine on any breeding farm, large or small. During the breeding season open mares should be teased regularly. Mares in estrus should be teased daily through their heats, so the intensity of their signs can be monitored and to double check that the mare teases out as expected. Mares thought to be in diestrus and/or early pregnancy (less than 40 days) should still be teased at least two to three times a week so short-cycling, possibly infected mares and mares which lose their pregnancies and unexpectedly return to estrus are not missed. Mare managers need to pay careful attention during the 14 to 18 days following an ovulation and to tease the mares daily so as not to miss the beginning of the next estrus period.

Mares which have been diagnosed as open (not pregnant) following an initial pregnancy ultrasound examination at 14 days and then fail to return to estrus warrant a second ultrasound examination. It is possible that she is pregnant and the embryo was overlooked at the initial exam because it was a little small for its gestational age or because the mare conceived on a second undetected ovulation a couple of days after the first ovulation (some stallions do produce extremely long-lived sperm). Likewise, it sometimes is difficult to determine accurately the early pregnancy status of mares which have numerous endometrial cysts. Again, if she fails to return to estrus it could indicate that the veterinarian's optimism is about to be rewarded by the detection of an enlarging embryo nestled amongst the cysts. (Cysts don't grow nor do they develop heart beats, so serial examinations are helpful and indicated.) Remember, too, that some pregnant mares can demonstrate mild signs of heat around 18 to 20 days; mares showing lukewarm signs definitely warrant a second look by a veterinarian before they are sent back to the breeding shed. It could also be that a mare that fails to tease back in at this time is truly not pregnant but has retained her CL and requires a shot of prostaglandin to get her back on the right track. A second timely examination by a veterinarian will save valuable time. Mares that have been given prostaglandin to bring them back into heat also warrant close daily teasing so as not to miss the start of the ensuing estrus period. Late winter anestrus and spring transitional mares also should be teased biweekly so as to get a handle on their progress. As always, keep good records.

As useful and important as it is to be able to regularly tease any mare intended for breeding, it is unfortunately not always possible. With the advent of shipped semen breeding by artificial insemination (AI) in those breeds whose registries permit its use many mare owners choose to breed their mares at home and do not have access to a teaser. Other farms, for various reasons, simply do not wish to have a teaser around. In still other instances, some mares simply do not display overt signs of behavioral estrus even though they are cycling normally (maiden mares, performance mares, mares with very young foals, etc., as previously discussed). In these instances more intensive observation of mares is required to detect subtle signs such as vulvar lengthening, clear and slight mucous vulvar discharge, increased restlessness, and vocalizations that all might indicate the mare is in estrus. Remember also to watch the mares' interactions with each other and people to detect whether they are demonstrating behavioral estrus.

Good record-keeping also can be a critical ally when trying to predict the occurrence of a heat period in protective mares who will not show heat well in the initial weeks following foaling. Recording the foaling date and then counting ahead 10 days to try to catch the foal heat (remember too the initial veterinary reproductive examination routinely performed on mares seven days after foaling also will initially help predict when the foal heat ovulation may occur) or counting further ahead 30 days from foaling to predict when the second estrus following foaling (the "30 day heat") should occur can be helpful in determining when a veterinarian should be scheduled to begin examining the mare rectally to facilitate breeding.

CHAPTER 5
Reproductive Examinations

Breeding mares is sometimes a humbling experience. Many mares seem to take perverse delight in outsmarting their managers and veterinarians, almost as if to say, "So you think you have it figured out? Watch this!" On average, mares will demonstrate receptivity for five to seven days, and we know they will likely ovulate during the last 24 to 48 hours of the heat. But accurately predicting exactly which day a given mare will ovulate can be difficult, especially if no records exist of her behavior and reproductive tract parameters on previous cycles.

One strategy to combat the "unknown" is to breed a mare every 48 hours during her heat cycle beginning on the second day of receptivity until she is no longer receptive to the stallion. This strategy is based on the knowledge that the average fertile stallion's semen will last in the mare's tract for at least 48 hours and that she will begin teasing out within 24 to 48 hours of ovulation. Therefore, breeding her every 48 hours during her heat increases the likelihood that there will be fertile sperm ready and waiting to fertilize the oocyte when the ovulated oocyte arrives in the oviduct. There are drawbacks to this approach, however, especially an increased likelihood of the mare developing a uterine infection. Semen is not sterile, and every breeding introduces contaminants and bacteria as well as sperm into the uterine lumen. Well conformed, healthy, young mares are adept at clearing this contamination in a timely fashion and are less likely to become infected as the result of breeding. Older mares, mares which have anatomical differences that incline them to pneumovagina and/or pooling vaginal urine or uterine fluid, and mares which have cervices that remain somewhat closed and fail to relax completely during estrus have a much more difficult time clearing contamination and are likely to develop an endometritis/uterine infection following breeding. For this latter class of mares, multiple breedings during a heat cycle are contraindicated.

> ## AT A GLANCE
>
> • Serial veterinary examinations can help determine when it is optimum to breed a mare.
>
> • During a rectal palpation, the vet can feel the ovaries, uterus, and cervix.
>
> • With ultrasound, sound waves give a visual image of the reproductive organs.
>
> • A speculum can help a vet see cyclical changes to the vagina and cervix.

With heavily booked stallions (especially in live cover scenarios) it might not be possible for a mare to get in to be bred more than once during a given estrus. Likewise, for logistical reasons, it sometimes is difficult to obtain numerous semen shipments when breeding artificially with shipped semen (it also becomes quite expensive), and frequently the number of available breeding doses is limited when dealing with frozen semen breedings. For these reasons, the breeding management goal for each mare is to breed her in front of, and as close to, the time of ovulation as possible to limit the number of breedings necessary.

When the timing is right on the mark (i.e., she is bred less than or equal to 48 hours before her ovulation), she will need to be bred only one time during the cycle, which is the ultimate goal of the breeding management. When breeding based solely on the mare's behavior, one effective strategy for some farms with exceptionally good and careful teasing management is to breed mares on the third day of their behavioral estrus, then once more on the fifth day if they continue to tease strongly. Because most mares ovulate sometime on or between the third and fifth day of estrus, this method can be quite effective for mares which show heat well and reliably. A more intensive breeding management approach is to combine serial teasing of a mare with serial rectal examination of her reproductive tract via direct palpation and ultrasonography. This method provides direct information about the structures on the mare's ovaries as well as the tonal quality of her uterus and cervix. The combination of this information and the mare's teasing behavior considered on multiple, sequential examinations throughout the heat provides a much more accurate picture of how the mare is progressing through her estrus and therefore a more valuable method of predicting her ovulation and the best time to breed her.

RECTAL PALPATION

Rectal palpation of a mare's reproductive tract involves the veterinarian carefully grasping and/or feeling the ovaries, uterus, and cervix through the rectal wall. The veterinarian has to stand adjacent to the hindquarters of the mare and place his or her well-lubricated and gloved hand and arm through the mare's anus and into her rectum. This is a potentially dangerous procedure for both the examiner and the mare, so it is important that proper restraint and good technique are employed to safeguard both participants. It never ceases to amaze me how well mares tolerate this procedure when the examiner takes the time to be gentle and unhurried, but understandably even the best-mannered mare may become a little goosey. A set of stocks is ideal for examining mares safely because stocks limit the mare's ability to swing side to side and forward and back, and afford the examiner some protection in the event the mare decides to kick out. It has been my experience that the majority of mares will readily accept being led into a set of stocks and stand quietly (even maidens) provided that they are handled with a little consideration. Not every farm has the luxury of a set of stocks, and in these instances mares may be restrained within a boxstall or by backing their hindquarters out partially through the stall doorway. Where a box stall is unavailable, tractable mares sometimes can be palpated effectively when

their free side is placed against a wall, again so that their ability to swing side to side is limited. If the mare is not in stocks, I prefer not to place anything behind her while I palpate her, although some practi-

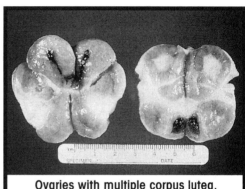

Ovaries with multiple corpus lutea.

tioners are more comfortable placing a bale of straw behind the mare's legs or palpating over a low Dutch type door. (The latter can be dangerous for the examiner if the half door is too tall. Should the mare suddenly decide to drop and tuck her hindquarters under herself, she will likely cause the examiner to break his or her arm on the edge of the half door.)

A handler should always stand at the mare's head to soothe, distract, and steady her during the examination. A halter and lead shank are obligatory, and many handlers prefer to restrain the mare further with the aid of a twitch. In my experience, many mares (regardless of their breed) do not require a twitch for this procedure as, judging by the mares' reactions, it does not appear to cause them pain or undue discomfort. I usually reserve the twitch for mares which continuously strain during examination or fidget excessively. Having said that, however, there are many mares which are well accustomed to a twitch and relax and stand readily with one applied by a person well-schooled in its proper application (too much unrelenting pressure on a twitch will actually cause horses to "blow up" — quite the opposite of the desired effect). Exceptionally nervous, fractious, or downright combative mares often benefit best with sedation (or "chemical attitude persuasion"). I like to sedate the mare before she can become excited, then work calmly and quietly while trying to make the experience as good as possible.

It is important to remember that some horses actually become more inclined to kick under the influence of Xylazine, so this drug often is used by veterinarians in combination with butorphenol or acepromazine to better keep the mare's feet on the ground. With repeated good experiences, some mares may no longer require sedation to permit examination. Safety, however, should always be of paramount concern, and safeguarded with whatever means are necessary (including not palpating the mare if it cannot be done safely for her or the examiner). Veterinarians have been seriously injured and even killed working on mares, and they are responsible not only for their own safety but that of the animal on which they are working.

The rectal wall of the horse is a thin and somewhat fragile structure that can be damaged and even torn during an examination. A tear rarely will occur in the hands of a careful, experienced examiner, but the possibility exists if the horse suddenly strains, moves, or jumps around unexpectedly. Rectal tears in horses are very serious. Horses do not deal well with the resultant peritonitis following fecal contamination of their abdomen, and the injury is likely to cause the horse's death due to the subsequent complications. In some instances, horses can recover provided surgical repair and medical treatment are prompt and aggressive, but it is far better to avoid the injury by using appropriate and judicious restraint.

ULTRASOUND

Ultrasound examination of the mare's reproductive tract uses sound waves to image the reproductive organs. Except for transabdominal imaging of the fetus during mid to late gestation, this examination also is performed rectally by introducing the probe into the mare's rectum in the hand of the examiner and systematically scanning the reproductive structures. B-mode, real time scanners typically are used to image the organs. High frequency sound waves are produced and emitted by a crystal within the probe. These sound waves then pass into the soft tissue structures and are either transmitted through the tissues or reflected back to the probe, depending on the tissue density. The sound waves readily pass through fluid and move through soft tissue densities to varying degrees, but are bounced back to the probe by bone and air. The image produced by the reflections of the sound waves reconstructs the reproductive organs in two-dimensional form in varying shades of white, gray, and black (i.e., B-mode stands for "brightness modality"). Fluid appears black, soft tissues appear in varying shades of gray, and bone and air appear white and cast a shadow over

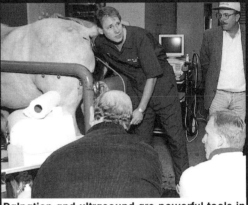

Palpation and ultrasound are powerful tools in determining a mare's status.

the image so that whatever is behind them cannot be imaged. The image is constructed and changes as the probe is passed over the structures so that the image is the "real time" reflection of what is being examined. As this procedure is being performed rectally, all of the precautions pertinent to rectal palpation apply here as well.

The combination of palpation and ultrasound of the reproductive tract is a powerful tool for determining the status of a mare. Follicles are readily identifiable both by palpation and ultrasound on a mare's ovaries. These fluid-filled ovarian structures project above the surface of the ovary proper and palpate much like a blister. Follicles first become identifiable to an experienced veterinarian's fingers when they are 10 to 20 mm in diameter and are readily identifiable when they are at the ovulatory size of 35 to 60 mm. As we have previously discussed, cycling mares typically produce one to two "waves" of developing follicles during a given 21-day estrous cycle.

From any given wave, a "dominant" follicle will emerge, and if this follicle's development should coincide with the regression of the previous cycle's corpus luteum (CL) — at approximately 14 to 17 days after ovulation — then that follicle will go on to become the ovulatory follicle for the next estrus period. This dominant follicle (or sometimes two follicles) is readily identifiable among the cohort of follicles because it has the largest diameter in the developing "wave," and frequently can be identified as early as 10 to 14 days into the diestrus period during which it is developing (i.e., four to eight days before the start of the next estrus period). Frequently the dominant follicle will be 25 to 30 mm in diameter at the beginning of the estrus period. A developing follicle typically will "grow" 3 to 5 mm in diameter each day. As the follicle approaches ovulation, it tends to soften and become fluctuant, and this change is readily apparent to the palpating veterinarian.

Likewise, the follicle also will begin to change in shape. The mare's follicles ovulate through the ovulation fossa on the ovary. The follicle maintains a somewhat spherical shape in the ovarian tissue up until the time when it is close to ovulating. As ovulation approaches (within 24 hours or less) the follicle begins to "cone down" toward the ovulation fossa and takes on a pear shape or grows a small "comet tail" toward the fossa. This change is not palpable; it is only discernible with an ultrasound machine.

One of the best predictors of impending ovulation in a mare is follicular size. In general, a mare will ovulate a follicle that is 35 to 60 mm in diameter (larger early in the physiological breeding season and smaller later), with the average mare most likely to ovulate a follicle when it is 40 to 50 mm in diameter. An experienced veterinarian can discern and identify these follicular diameters. An ultrasound machine increases the accuracy of these assessments and gives the examiner additional information about the appearance of the follicle. Ultrasound also can readily distinguish when there are two smaller follicles "back to back" that may palpate like one large follicle, thereby foiling the mare's attempts to fool her examiner. In general, then, when a mare's dominant follicle reaches a diameter of 35 to 40 mm, it is a reasonable "guesstimate" to say that she is within 24 to 48 hours of ovulation. This prediction can be further modified based on how the follicle looks and feels, how strongly the mare is teasing in, what her uterine and cervical tone feel like, the amount of uterine edema the mare is displaying, and, just as importantly, what the mare has done during previous ovulations.

Complete, accurate records are a useful reference when a veterinarian and manager are following any mare, especially when dealing with mares which like to ovulate smaller diameter follicles, double ovulate, and/or bring up a 45 to 50 mm follicle and then "hang there" for 24 to 72 hours before going on to ovulate. For example, if I am dealing with a mare which fooled us by ovulating a 30 to 35 mm follicle on the previous cycle before we could breed her, I am much more likely to get some semen into her "early" the next time (provided everything else looks all right) when she is showing a 30 mm follicle, in the hopes of catching her at her own game.

In the first few hours after ovulation, there is a palpable crater or depression on the ovary where the ovulated follicle had been. Touching this area can be painful to the mare. Occasionally a mare will react to the palpation of this site by jumping about or even kicking. But most mares will merely tense up as the examiner grasps the ovary, and there will be a discernible, slight quivering in the mare's flank as the ovary is handled. Within 12 to 24 hours of ovulation this sensitivity disappears, and the ovulated, collapsed follicle has filled back up to a greater or lesser extent with blood to form a corpus hemorrhagicum (CH). This structure is usually the same size or smaller than the previous follicle but will have a thicker, "meaty" texture to it rather than the smooth, tense, fluid feel of the follicle. The hemorrhage into the collapsed follicle can be extensive, and the mare may have a 60 to 90 mm hematoma where the follicle used to be, but this occurs infrequently during the physiological breeding season.

The collapsed, recently ovulated follicle is discernible with an ultrasound machine (especially if the examiner knows there was a large follicle present just a few hours before), as a bright, echogenic, and lacy CH. As the CH begins to organize and "luteinize" to form the CL proper, the structure shrinks and consolidates so that it no longer projects above the ovary's surface and therefore becomes increasingly difficult to identify by palpation alone as the mare progresses into her diestrous period. Remember the mare continues to bring up one or two waves of follicles throughout the entire estrous cycle, and it is quite possible for a mare to have a fairly large follicle (30 mm +) along with a CL during her diestrus period. Therefore, a large follicle does not guarantee that a mare is in heat. The presence of a large follicle needs to be considered with all the behavioral and examination findings.

An experienced veterinarian often has a pretty good idea if a mare has a CL on an ovary based on palpation alone. Indications include increased uterine and cervical tone and one ovary that is somewhat larger than the other with a larger diameter to one pole but no discernible follicle (this is where information about how the mare is presently teasing is particularly useful). However, examination of the ovaries with an ultrasound or measurement of circulating levels of progesterone in the mare's blood will be necessary to confirm and identify the presence of an active or developing CL. The progesterone assay will in all likelihood require 24 to 72+ hours before the results are known. Mature CLs, however, might be identified with a high degree of accuracy on the spot with an ultrasound examination.

Under the influence of the steroid hormones (estrogen and progesterone), the mare's uterine and cervical tone and texture undergo dramatic changes from one phase of the estrous cycle to the next. These palpable and imaged changes are valuable pieces of information that the veterinarian uses to fine tune his or her predictions of when ovulation is likely to occur. During diestrus, the progesterone produced by the mature CL causes the cervix to become tightly closed and the uterus to feel toned up and somewhat tubular. These changes are amplified during early pregnancy. During diestrus there normally is no uterine edema discernible on ultrasound, the uterine image is a homogenous gray and the horns are distinctly circular on a cross-sectional image. At the end of diestrus in the non-pregnant mare, the CL regresses in response to the uterine release of prostaglandin.

As progesterone levels fall, the mare's tract is free to respond to the increasing levels of estrogen being produced by the developing, dominant follicle. The uterine tone loses its tubularity, and the uterus becomes softer and somewhat limp in the veterinarian's hand. During the early estrus period in particular, edema begins to fill the tissues of the endometrium, and the folds become more prominent. On palpation these edematous folds also cause the uterus to feel somewhat thicker and flatter but still soft, and the folds can be discerned on deep palpation of the uterus.

On ultrasound, the edema-filled endometrial folds give the cross-sectional view of the uterine horns a "sliced orange or wagon wheel" appearance. As the mare progresses into her estrus and the time of ovulation approaches, the amount of edema in her uterus begins to decrease and the uterus becomes subjectively thinner, but even softer and more draping. This loss of edema is readily identifiable on serial ultrasound examinations, and the shape of the uterine horns on cross-sectional view increasingly lose their circularity and begin to conform somewhat to the pressure of the examining probe and flatten. Many mares at this time also will have small amounts (10 mm or less) of trace, clear, free fluid in their uterine lumen that is identifiable on ultrasound examination. Small amounts are normal, and often these mares will also have a slight, clear, thin mucous discharge from their vulvae. Large pools of free uterine fluid and/or cloudy fluid, however, indicate that the mare might have an infection and requires a closer look and possibly treatment before she is bred. Likewise, aspirated air in the uterine lumen is readily imaged with ultrasound and quickly identifies a mare which had what appeared to be normal perineal conformation when she was in diestrus, but begins to "windsuck" when her tissues relax during estrus and therefore needs a Caslick's procedure. As the mare progresses into and through the heat, the cervix demonstrates a dramatic, palpable change as it "shortens" and becomes thicker with edema early on in estrus as compared to its diestrus feel. As ovulation draws closer, the edema is lost and the cervix becomes softer and loses its normal palpable shape, becoming flatter and more difficult to discern. This latter finding taken together with the described pre-ovulatory changes in the uterus and a 40 to 50 mm follicle on an ovary and no discernible CL are good indications that this mare needs some semen.

A note of caution and again a reminder to keep good records: These estrus uterine and cervical changes are demonstrated in most mares and will be reliable from cycle to cycle in most cases. But some mares routinely do not demonstrate much uterine edema, or do not seem to relax their cervices to the same degree as other mares just before ovulating. Good records will identify those mares which bear particularly close scrutiny during breeding.

SPECULUM EXAM

Lastly, these cyclic changes to the mare's tract (in particular her cervix) can be seen by a veterinarian using a vaginal speculum. The information that can be gathered by "specking a mare" is very useful. This technique is routinely used during early estrus, especially in those instances when palpation alone (without the additional benefit of ultrasound) is being used. The pallor and moistness of the vaginal mucosa shifts with the phase of the mare's cycle. During diestrus, the mucosa is pale and somewhat dry and tacky (this finding is particularly pronounced when the mare is pregnant). During estrus the mucosa is increasingly a rich, moist pink. Conversely, any mare experiencing a vaginal irritation or an infection deeper within the tract will typically have a mucosa that is reddened and "angry" looking. Accumulations of urine (many mares only pool urine when they are in estrus) or exudate in the floor of the cranial vagina are readily identified as is fecal material and/or froth that indicate a mare is suffering from pneumovagina or a small, previously undetected recto-vaginal fistula.

The cervix undergoes a typical visual transformation throughout the cycle following the same previously described palpable pattern. During diestrus the cervix is pale and tightly closed, and the external cervical os projects into the vaginal lumen from the cranial wall of the vagina up off of the vaginal floor. As the mare enters estrus the cervix pinkens, softens, and begins to relax. The folds of the external cervical os begin to swell with edema, and the cervix starts to look like a moist "rosebud." As ovulation gets closer, the cervix continues to relax until it "melts" onto the floor of the vagina and is open with mucosal folds draped over the opening.

A veterinarian can identify any abnormal redness or discharges coming from the cervical os (and therefore the uterine lumen) by looking directly at the cervix. Speculum examination also can identify previous foaling injuries to the cervix such as tears and bruising (the former are often easier felt than seen). In normal estrus mares, the degree of cervical relaxation seen on speculum examination, taken in conjunction with rectal palpation findings, helps the examining veterinarian more accurately predict how close a given mare is from ovulating.

CHAPTER 6

Natural Matings

In the typical domestic setting, the optimal goal of following a mare closely through her heat period is to time her actual breeding so it will occur in advance of and within 24 to 48 hours of ovulation. The objective is to breed her only one time during a single estrus period. The actual breeding can be accomplished naturally or artificially, depending primarily on the regulations for registering the resulting offspring.

Many breed registries now permit the registration of foals resulting from artificial insemination and embryo transfer. Some, like The Jockey Club registry for Thoroughbreds, only allow the registration of foals which result from a natural mating or "live cover." Many breed organizations which permit artificial breeding impose a strict set of criteria (i.e., they might permit artificial insemination with fresh semen but not frozen or shipped). Therefore, breeders should consult with a given organization before a planned mating so that the breed organization's rules will be followed accurately.

Pasture breeding and hand breeding fall within the context of natural mating. Breeding by artificial insemination (AI) involves 1) using semen which has been freshly collected from the sire; 2) using collected, cooled, and transported semen; or 3) using frozen semen stored in liquid nitrogen which is thawed just prior to breeding.

PASTURE BREEDING

As the term implies, pasture breeding involves natural mating in a pasture and most closely resembles the wild state in that it leaves estrus detection, timing, and frequency of breeding up to the mare and stallion. When the stallion is fertile, the conception rates are typically quite high (85%+). Left to their own devices, the estrus mare and stallion interact continuously throughout the day and night. During the early stages of estrus, mares can be ambivalent or even hostile toward the stallion and typically will not allow themselves to be mounted. As ovulation approaches, however, the mare's receptivity intensifies and the breeding pair frequently will copulate every few hours around the clock.

> ### AT A GLANCE
>
> • Natural mating or "live cover" includes pasture and hand breeding.
>
> • Due to possible injury, valuable mares and stallions typically are not used to pasture breed.
>
> • Well-managed breeding sheds can have a crew of up to five people to assist a breeding.
>
> • A mare should be restrained during a live cover as a safety precaution.

Pasture breeding has distinct advantages: there is little need for human interference other than to observe the goings on closely, maintain good records, and conduct regular pregnancy checks to identify pregnancy and to gauge gestational age. This system works well when the players (i.e., the stallion and the mares) are maintained in a stable, companionable group. The potential for injury to the mares and especially the stallion in this system is obvious and for this reason it is not typically used with very valuable animals. Nor is this system practical or safe when outside mares are presented for breeding. Reshuffling the group dynamics with the constant introduction and removal of mares creates an unstable environment for all the horses, especially when mares have foals by their sides. Disease transmission between resident and transient horses also poses a concern. For these reasons, many managers prefer to hand mate individuals.

HAND BREEDING

Hand breeding involves the mare and stallion being presented and mated to one another in a structured setting where handlers control and direct the actions of the two horses without getting in the way. Hand breeding requires professionalism, good horsemanship, and common sense to avoid injury to horse and human. It also involves monitoring the routines, reactions, and idiosyncrasies of the horses, and taking steps to prevent disease.

In the author's opinion, hand breeding a stallion and a mare requires a minimum of three people in the breeding shed. A

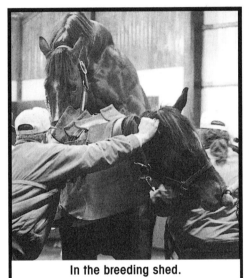

In the breeding shed.

mare handler is required to hold, calm, support, and restrain the mare as necessary. A stallion handler controls and directs the actions of the stallion. This individual should have a good rapport and working relationship with the stallion. The third person acts as a "swing man" of sorts who holds up a mare's front leg (with a leg strap) to discourage her from kicking as the stallion mounts, or stands next to the hind end of the mare to assist or steady the horses. The "swing man" might pull the mare's tail out of the way, help guide the stallion's penis into the mare's vulva, place a steadying hand on the hindquarters to help the mare and stallion maintain their balance and position, position and hold a breeding roll if needed, or catch a "dismount sample" of semen as the stallion withdraws from the mare's vulva.

Many well-managed breeding sheds use a crew of five to supervise and assist the breeding: a stallion handler, a mare handler, one person to steady the mare and hold up her front leg during mounting and initial intromission, one person to pull the mare's tail out of the way and introduce a breeding roll as needed, and one to help guide the stallion's penis into the mare and catch the dismount sample. Regardless of the number of people involved, each member of the breeding crew knows his or her job and works in concert with the others, relying upon one another's horsemanship and skills to keep everyone safe. The activities within the breeding shed can rapidly erupt into an explosive situation. The breeding crew should be composed of experienced individuals who are excellent horsemen.

Beginners should read all they can, but the knowledge and experience needed can only be acquired through firsthand experience under the tutelage of veteran horsemen. People just starting out in the breeding business should find a breeding farm which has excellent breeding shed management and seek to "apprentice" before trying to breed horses on their own. Chances are good that small breeders (those with only a few mares) will not be breeding their mare to their own stallion. The mare instead will go to an "outside" stallion for breeding, and she will most likely be the responsibility of the stallion's breeding shed management during her visit.

Most well-run breeding sheds handle the mare themselves and only permit the mare owner or agent to watch from a safe observation area. However, even if asked or offered the opportunity to handle your own mare during the cover, the mare owner or agent should only do so if he or she has the experience. If you are "green" in this area, please be honest with yourself and the stallion's personnel. Do not place yourself, the people around you, and the horses at risk.

A breeding session should be performed efficiently. The environment should be calm, professional, and free of distractions. Breeding horses should never be rushed or frantic, but well-planned to ensure safety and success.

The breeding shed itself should be large enough to allow a safety margin that provides everyone ample "running room" for escape should the activities go awry. The ceiling should be plenty high so that the stallion does not hit his head on anything while he is on his hind legs. The footing must be secure so the horses do not slip. The floor should be dust free with good drainage and have some degree of cushion so that if a horse falls it is not as likely to be severely injured. A large grass paddock that is safely fenced (a wire fence is not appropriate) is adequate in good weather but a covered enclosure is preferable. Padded walls also are a nice feature to have in place.

During a live cover the mare and stallion by definition are in direct contact. Therefore, disease transmission between the two horses is a valid concern. Equine viral arteritis, contagious equine metritis, and coital exanthema (herpes-virus type III) are all transmitted venereally. The mare's vulva and vagina and the stallion's penis and semen are not sterile and contamination and transmission of normal flora as well as pathogenic bacteria can occur during coitus. Many stallion managers require that mares have a negative uterine culture prior to breeding to prevent the futile breeding of an infected mare and to protect the stallion from potential infection from a pathogenic bacterium.

Cleanliness and proper preparation of the mare's and stallion's external genitalia for breeding further reduce the possibility of contaminating the mare's uterus with fecal organisms and penile smegma. The mare's tail is wrapped prior to breeding. This not only aids in cleanliness but also keeps her long tail hairs out of the way during breeding so they don't lacerate the stallion's penis. The mare's hindquarters, perineum, and vulva are washed thoroughly with a mild soap and clean water, taking extra care to make sure that the vulva is free of contaminating dirt and fecal material and that all of the soap is carefully and completely rinsed away (soap is spermicidal!). It is impossible to "sterilize" the mare prior to breeding, and the use of strong disinfectants is actually contraindicated as repeated use of these substances disrupts the normal flora of the mare's skin and instead promotes the growth and colonization of pathogenic organisms such as *Pseudomonas* and *Klebsiella*. For this reason, the stallion's penis is routinely washed only with clean water before and/or after breeding. Strict cleanliness between horses and the use of disposable tail wraps, bucket liners, wash cotton, and gloves further reduces the likelihood of spreading contamination and organisms between mares as well.

RESTRAINT DEVICES

The art of stallion handling and stallion management is beyond the scope of this text and will only be addressed where it applies to the mare's management. From this perspective we will now turn to some of the more common pieces of equipment and practices used during the course of live covering of mares. Restraint of the mare during a live cover is a practical safety consideration. Most mares in good standing heat will do just that, stand still and allow themselves to be bred. However, even the most willing of mares can become agitated or frightened during the process and it is imperative that the mare not topple the stallion by moving about while he is mounted or kicking out with her hind feet, especially when he is at his most vulnerable (i.e., as he is exposing his belly and genitals to her hind feet as he raises up to mount). In addition, the mare should not have leeway to kick, strike, or run over any of the handlers. For this reason, some mares are restrained using a twitch or a chain shank applied over their noses or their upper gums.

To decrease the severity of a kick or prevent one, some handlers will apply a leg strap to one front leg, lift the leg while the stallion mounts and enters the mare, then release the leg once the stallion is in place so that the mare can stabilize herself and support the weight of the stallion. Breeding hobbles are sometimes used instead of the leg strap, but they should be used with the utmost caution and only on those mares which have been trained to accept them. There is a very real danger of the mare and even the stallion becoming tangled up in the hobble ropes if the mare struggles. Many mares react violently to the hobble restraints on their hind legs and panic at the feel of the restricted movement. It is imperative, therefore, that a mare be introduced to the hobbles slowly and patiently well in advance of their use in a breeding situation so that she is completely comfortable wearing and walking in them. The surest way to get into a horrific "train wreck" is to hustle a maiden mare into a breeding shed, throw on a set of hobbles, then confront her with a lusty stallion (not a good idea!). One last piece of equipment commonly used in an effort literally to "soften the blow" of a potential kick is padded booties that are placed over the mare's hind hooves. Again, it is imperative to allow the mare a chance to become accustomed to the feel and sound of these boots; otherwise, she is likely to kick like a mule in an effort to get them off and bolt.

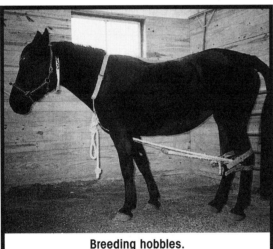

Breeding hobbles.

In addition to the mare restraints, other equipment designed to protect the mare from injury also can be used during the course of a cover. Many stallions will stabilize themselves on the mare's back by taking hold of her crest or poll with their teeth. Some stallions are overly aggressive with this type of biting and others are downright nasty and like to savage a mare's neck. Not only is this painful for the poor mare (who could blame her for not wanting to stand in such a situation), but such bites can cause severe lacerations. For this reason, many breeding sheds routinely place a heavy canvas or leather cover or "shroud" over the mare's poll, neck, and withers. These breeding shrouds are attached with straps affixed to her halter and a surcingle that goes around her girth. The cover usually will have flaps attached to its surface that the stallion can bite if he so chooses and the mare remains unharmed.

A breeding roll is a padded tube attached to a stick handle that is used to prevent lacerations or rupture of the mare's vaginal wall by the stallion's penis during the course of a natural breeding. Some stallions are extremely well endowed when it comes to penile length and/or are extremely vigorous upon entering and thrusting within a mare's vagina. There are also mares which have somewhat shorter vaginal cavities than average or are proportionately smaller than the stallion's penile length because they are a proportionately smaller horse. In these instances the mare is at real risk for potentially serious injury to her vaginal wall. For instance, if the stallion completely ruptures the cranial vaginal wall, he will penetrate her peritoneal cavity and the mare will be at real risk of developing peritonitis or of herniating her intestine through the rent. Use of the breeding roll lessens the likelihood of such an injury occurring by preventing the stallion from fully penetrating the mare. The breeding roll is slipped above the stallion's penis and between the hindquarters of the mare and stallion after the stallion has penetrated the mare. In this way the stallion is held a good six to 10 inches out of the mare.

Even with the use of a breeding roll, however, injury is still possible and any sign of blood in the dismount sample, on the stallion's penis as he withdraws, or in or on the vulva of the mare should be investigated immediately. Many times a mare might only be bruised, but can suffer tears on a subsequent cover during the same estrus if the injury is left undiscovered.

A breeding stitch is sometimes put into place in the vulva of a mare to protect a caslicksed vulva from being torn open and apart during coitus. Many mares which have been caslicksed still have a large enough vaginal opening to permit penetration and breeding by a stallion. A breeding stitch is a heavy gauge loop of suture material that is placed at the bottom most aspect of the healed together or stitched together vulvar lips. As the remaining open portion of the ventral vulva is spread apart, the breeding stitch takes up the tension before it is applied to the scar or suture line. By taking up the tension in this fashion, the breeding stitch prevents the Caslick's repair from being stretched and torn open during the course of the cover.

It is imperative that each mare's vulva be thoroughly examined prior to breeding live cover, first to check for the presence of a Caslick's, and second, to check to see whether such a mare is open enough to permit breeding or whether she needs to have her Caslick's partially opened or completely opened prior to the breeding. It is the stallion manager's decision whether to breed a mare with a breeding stitch in place or to remove it and open the mare's Caslick's. The heavy gauge suture of the stitch can severely damage a stallion's penis if it is in the way so it is important to assess the situation carefully beforehand. Always check every mare for the presence of a Caslick's repair prior to breeding live cover. Some mares are sutured quite tightly and this will prevent the stallion from being able to penetrate the mare at all. I have had more than one call from a frantic owner concerned that a stallion was unable to breed a mare only to find a Caslick's in place the moment I lifted the mare's tail and took a close look at her vulva.

Lastly, it is important we don't forget the handlers themselves. There are some wonderful chest protectors on the market these days, and a strong argument can be made for wearing such devices while breeding horses. The same can be said for wearing gloves when handling the shanks on the stallion and mare, but these items are a matter of personal preference. In the author's opinion, however, protective headgear should be a mandatory piece of equipment for any and all persons who are managing and participating in any part of the breeding shed activities. Whether intentional or accidental, a horse's hoof striking a person's skull can do a lot

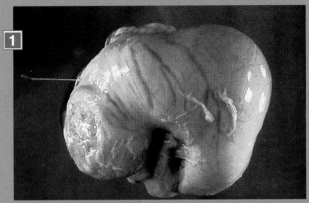

1) equine ovary with a large follicle;
2) ovarian corpora hemorrhagicum.

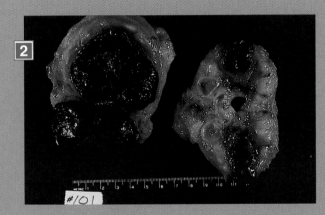

3) endometrial biopsy.

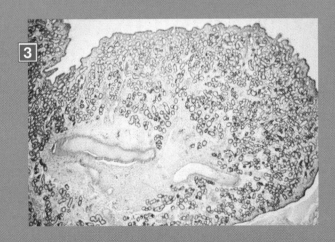

1) Adjusting a phantom mount to fit the stallion; 2) a stallion mounts the phantom, and his semen is collected.

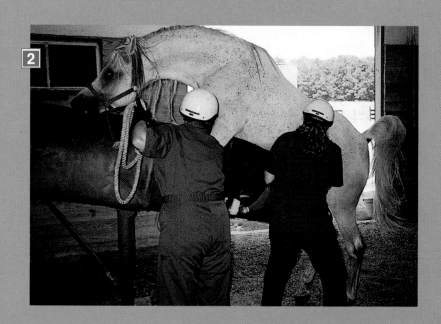

3) The semen in a container at the base of an artificial vagina; 4) the semen is prepared for shipment.

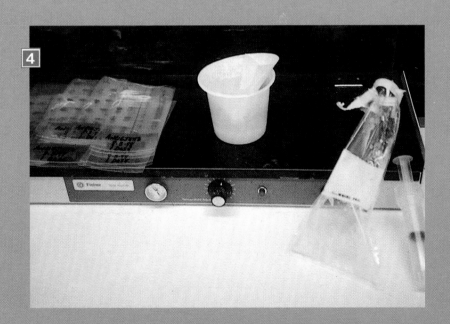

1) The cooled semen is packed (box transport system); 2) and placed in a container. The collector provides pertinent information such as stallion's name, date semen collected, and destination (Equitaner system).

3) Some carriers offer same day service; 4) with cooled semen, time is of the essence. Transported semen loses its effectiveness after 24 hours, and mares need to be inseminated ideally 12 to 24 hours before ovulating.

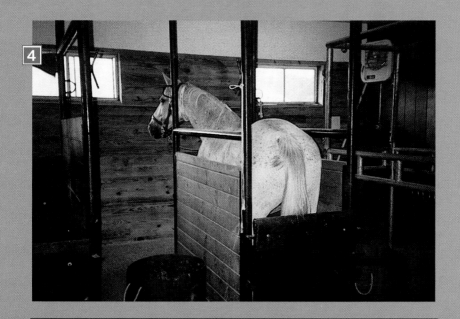

1 & 2) A pipette is used to inseminate the mare with the transported semen. The inseminator inserts the pipette with a gloved arm and hand.

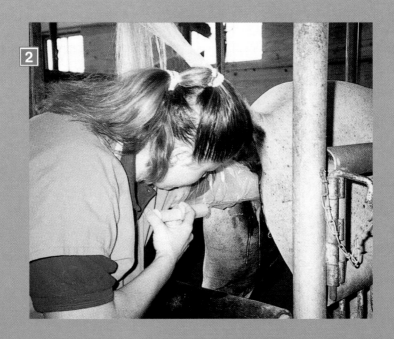

Embryo transfer involves flushing an embryo from the uterus of a donor mare (1); and transferring it (2) to the uterus of a recipient mare, which carries the developing fetus to term.

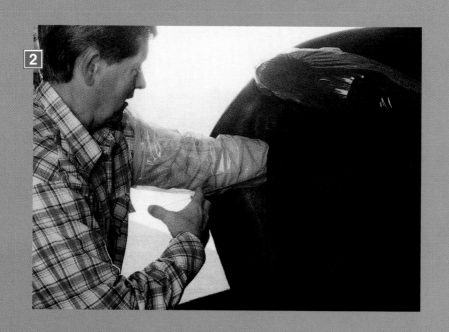

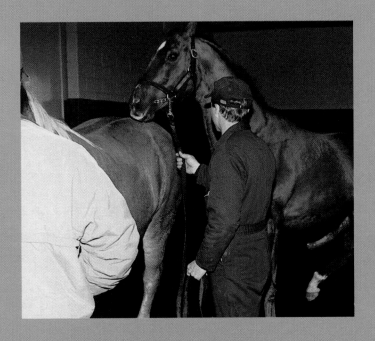

Live cover breedings require sufficient personnel and a
safe, secure breeding shed.

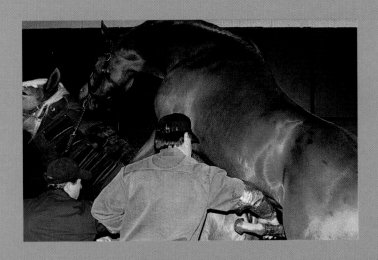

of damage. There is no reason to risk serious brain injury or death, and it is sheer arrogance and foolishness to ignore the possibility of an accident. By the very nature of the cover the stallion has to be up in the air mounting and in some cases dismounting. Distractions happen; horses get startled. Sometimes they strike out unexpectedly. No matter how experienced you are, you can still be at risk, and it only takes a split second.

The basic components of the cover require the stallion to become aroused, achieve an erection, mount the mare in a controlled fashion, achieve intromission, thrust and ejaculate, then dismount. The mare needs to remain cooperative and calm throughout. Specific routines designed to accomplish this in a clean and safe fashion will differ slightly from shed to shed, and can vary to suit the individual stallion and mare involved. In some shed routines the stallion is initially presented to the mare and teased in a controlled fashion so that he achieves an erection. He then is turned away from the mare to a designated corner so that his erect penis can be washed and dried prior to the cover. Other sheds only wash the stallion's penis after the dismount. In some instances mares are too tall for a given stallion to breed without some adjustments. Some sheds have a depression in the floor, or the mare faces downhill on a gradual slope so the stallion can reach her. Some mares will stand well as long as no one tries to twitch them; others dance about until the twitch is applied. Mare handling methods in these cases are adjusted as required.

Some stallions need no formal teasing time and enter the shed ready to go. Other stallions require careful teasing and patient handling to become aroused enough to breed the mare. Some stallions have decided preferences for mare color, teasing at the mare's head as opposed to her hindquarters, or having a moving, reactive mare to interact with as opposed to a mare who is stock still. It is important that the overall routine for a given horse remains consistent. In this manner the horses (the stallions in particular) become comfortable and relaxed within the routine, and the cover can be accomplished efficiently within a set order of events.

During the cover it also becomes necessary to verify that the stallion has indeed ejaculated. If he does not, then the mare obviously has not been bred. It is not unusual for some stallions to require more than one mount to ejaculate (although most stallions can be trained to ejaculate consistently on the first jump provided their individual needs are met). Normal stallions with good libido and no ejaculatory failure problems generally will ejaculate upon entering the mare after approximately seven thrusts. The ejaculation of the sperm is achieved in several distinct pulses or jets of sperm-rich fluid being passed

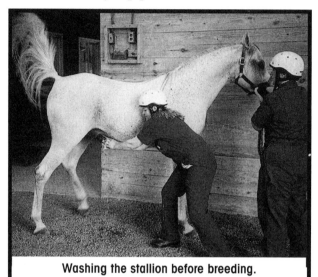

Washing the stallion before breeding.

through the penile urethra. As ejaculation occurs, many stallions' tails will jerk up and down. This ejaculatory motion is termed "flagging" and is readily visible to observers when it occurs. The ejaculatory pulses also can be felt by the handler if he or she is palpating the base of the stallion's penis while the horse is servicing the mare. Many stallions do not mind having their penises handled in this fashion while they are breeding, and some actually find the addition of manual pressure quite stimulatory. Other stallions resent having their penises handled at this moment and are distracted from ejaculating.

Once a stallion ejaculates, he frequently will relax and actually take a few moments just to drape over the back of the mare before dismounting. As the stallion dismounts and withdraws, the end of his penis (the glans) will appear quite enlarged and flared. This "belling" occurs as a result of the erectile bodies within the glans becoming distended by the ejaculatory pulses. Therefore, a penis that is belled out during dismount can be another indication that the stallion has ejaculated. So can demeanor. If he remains calm, relaxed, and even a little drowsy with no further interest in the mare, then he probably has ejaculated. If he remains alert and very interested in the mare, and he returns to an erect state within a couple of moments, then he probably has not.

Lastly, an objective measure of whether the stallion has ejaculated is to collect a sample of the fluid dripping from the stallion's penis as he withdraws from the mare (a "dismount sample") and examine it under the microscope for the presence of sperm. The mere presence of fluid is not enough to say the stallion has ejaculated as many stallions produce a lot of pre-ejaculatory secretions while thrusting, but these do not contain sperm. Only the use of a microscope can ascertain this. It is important to mention that the presence of sperm in the dismount samples only allows the examiner to confirm that the stallion has ejaculated, along with some gross visual observations on the sample itself (i.e., is there blood or urine present). The dismount sample does not allow the examiner to assess the semen's quality. The sperm in the dismount sample merely represents "the dregs" of the semen deposited, not the overall sperm parameters of the ejaculate.

The bottom line in a live cover management system is that the mare ultimately has to stand and permit herself to be bred. She must be in estrus and ready to ovulate. Teasing the mare prior to breeding is an integral part of the breeding shed routine. Uncooperative mares which do not tease well should be re-examined rectally by a veterinarian prior to attempting to breed them to be sure that they are truly at the correct point in their cycle.

Occasionally mares are presented for breeding which are not very close to ovulation or are not even in estrus. These might be mares which have not been teased at all, but only palpated one time without any follow-up and the presence of a large follicle was misinterpreted. (It is difficult to tell sometimes by a single palpation whether a mare is coming in or going out of heat. It is important to follow mares serially and use an ultrasound if needed to help make these determinations, especially when the mare is not being teased at home.)

Another possibility is that the mare is not teasing well prior to breeding because she is in fact pregnant (approximately 18 to 20 days of gestation), but she has a large follicle and half teases in anyway and so has misled her managers (rectal palpation and visual inspection of the mare's cervix and an ultrasound of the mare's uterus quickly will identify pregnancy). A mare which has recently ovulated (i.e., within the last 12 to 24 hours) might not tease in strongly or at all, and so will not stand as well at the time she is presented. At the opposite end is the mare which is presenting early in her estrus and is more than 24 to 48 hours away from ovulating.

Occasionally a heavily booked stallion cannot service a mare at her ideal time. Instead she has to go in early or not at all. A mare like this might not be at her most receptive. Just to make life interesting, some mares do not tease well when presented for breeding even though the timing is absolutely perfect for their impending ovulation and they should be red hot receptive. There is that subclass of normally cycling mares which do not demonstrate signs of heat because of poor socialization, prior exposure to anabolic steroids, dominance, or some unknown factor. Maiden mares sometimes are frightened by the new sights, smells, and sounds of their first trip to the breeding shed, and will not show heat well. There are also those mares which show heat very well at home, but are uncomfortable away from home and do not tease when they reach the breeding shed. Some mares have a decided stallion preference and will act receptive to one stallion but not another.

Lastly, mares with young foals frequently are too protective to show heat. If the breeding shed is close to the mare's farm the foals often are left at home under supervision for the one to two hours that the mare will be away. The absence of a foal can make it easier on the breeding shed personnel. Without their foals by their sides many mares are more willing to listen to their estrogen, but some mares have the opposite reaction and are too agitated to cooperate. These ready but reluctant mares will require a more patient and creative approach.

Some farms train their maiden mares by allowing a teaser stallion to mount them. The teaser stallion wears a "breeding apron" which covers his penis and thus prevents him from actually breeding the mare. A mare which knows what to expect is not as likely to blow up while being bred for the first time, possibly injuring a valuable stallion or the handlers in the process. Many stallion managers likewise will test jump mares in this fashion immediately prior to their being bred to their valuable stallion if there is any question about the mare's receptivity and her willingness to stand. Some dominant mares initially will try to intimidate a stallion, but then submit once the stallion is mounted. By sending the teaser stallion into the "lion's den" first, the mare is given the chance to demonstrate she will behave. An experienced jump teaser is usually quite good at taking care of himself and avoiding injury. Ultimately it is the stallion manager's call whether a mare will be covered.

Chemical sedation is a last alternative to try on a ready but unwilling mare. A fine balance has to be reached between sedating the mare to the point at which she will quietly stand but remain balanced enough to support the weight of the mounted stallion. Only an experienced veterinarian should administer sedation in these instances, and it should be noted that even a sedated mare might "wake up" in a hurry. In those breeds that permit its use the simplest and safest way of breeding a recalcitrant estrus mare is to bypass the natural cover and breed her via artificial insemination.

CHAPTER 7

Artificial Insemination

Breeding with artificial insemination offers a number of advantages. First there is the safety issue. From the standpoint of the stallion and the handlers especially, it is far safer to collect semen from a trained jump mare (or even better, an artificial phantom mount) than to undertake a live cover with an unknown mare. Secondly there is the issue of contamination. Breeding is a dirty business no matter how careful the managers are about making sure the mare and stallion are properly cleaned and prepared beforehand. The potential for cross contamination between the mare and stallion exists any time they are in direct contact. AI eliminates the need for the stallion to be in direct contact with the mare he is breeding. Therefore, it eliminates the possibility of the stallion contracting something from the mare.

From the mare's perspective it is without a doubt the cleanest breeding option available if performed correctly. Semen extenders often include an antibiotic, the addition of which can lessen the likelihood of bacterial contamination of the mare's tract through the semen itself. (Remember, however, antibiotics do not protect against viral contamination of the semen.) Also, careful manual insemination with semen results in less overall contamination of the mare's uterus than does natural breeding. Thirdly, a breeding dose of semen has fewer sperm in it than does the average total ejaculate from a stallion. The mare's inflammatory response following AI breeding is therefore likely to be less than when natural covered.

Another advantage of AI breeding is that it increases the breeding efficiency of the stallion as a number of mares can be bred using a single ejaculate. The average number of breeding doses available per ejaculate ranges from five to more than 10.

AI is also a means of extending the breeding life of valuable stallions which have musculo-skeletal, neurological, or behavioral problems that prevent them from performing live covers. Lastly, it allows close monitoring of a stallion's semen quality as every ejaculate can (and should) be fully evaluated.

> ## AT A GLANCE
>
> • Artificial insemination is safer for the horses and their handlers.
>
> • Transported semen increases a stallion's availability to mares.
>
> • Breeding a mare via AI requires excellent management and organization.
>
> • Proper handling of semen during collection, extension, and insemination is vital to the semen's fertility.

Breeding artificially with transported semen has the additional benefits of eliminating the need to transport and board mares and their foals away from their home farms. Transported semen also has the advantage of increasing a stallion's availability to mares which live far from where he stands (i.e., he might live on the West Coast and she in the Northeast). In this way, regional gene pools can remain more diverse and mare owners have an opportunity to breed to superior stallions which would otherwise be unavailable to their breeding program.

With the good, however, there is always the bad. Any time man steps in and substitutes for, or changes, the natural occurrence of equine reproductive events, the degree of reproductive management must intensify to ensure success. When you are breeding horses artificially, the semen handling on the stallion's end must be done correctly to safeguard the semen's fertility. In addition, anytime you remove the stallion from the equation, it becomes the responsibility of the mare's connections to ensure that the mare is in fact in heat and at her optimal readiness to be bred.

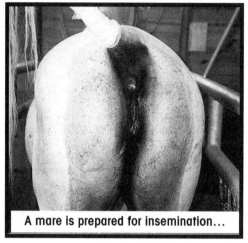

A mare is prepared for insemination...

Also bear in mind that the longer fresh chilled semen has to survive outside of the stallion's tract before insemination, or the more the sperm cells are manipulated in order to facilitate freezing, the less fertile the semen becomes. Sperm motility, longevity, and its ability to fertilize an oocyte begin to suffer. To make matters worse, the semen of some stallions does not ship and/or freeze well. The bottom line is this: using AI to breed a mare requires excellent breeding management and organization.

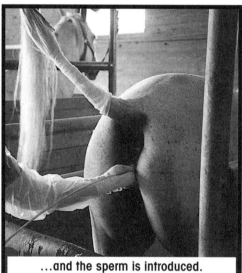

...and the sperm is introduced.

The technique for actually inseminating a mare with semen artificially is fairly straightforward. The mare is restrained as needed, ideally in a set of stocks, much the same as she is for rectal palpation. Her tail is wrapped with disposable gauze and her perineum and vulva are thoroughly washed and rinsed free of dirt, fecal material, and soap residues. Individual, disposable cotton, a mild soap, and clean, preferably warm water work best. Once the cleaning is finished, the vulva and perineum are carefully patted dry with a clean paper towel or wrung out cotton (water is spermicidal).

The veterinarian then puts on a sterile sleeve and glove. A long, sterile inseminating rod (pipette or "insemination gun" depending on the type of semen being used) is carefully placed in the vet's gloved hand. Sterile, non-spermicidal lubricant is placed on the back of the glove or sleeve. The veterinarian then introduces his or her arm with the pipette through the vulva, into the mare's vestibule, and further inward to the cranial vagina. Once positioned into the cranial vagina, the vet carefully feels for the external os of the mare's cervix. Once the cervix has been located, the tip of the inseminating pipette is carefully guided through the mare's cervix until it is just inside of the mare's uterus. Once the pipette is properly positioned, the semen (which has either been preloaded in a syringe attached to the pipette or which is in straws loaded into the "insemination gun") is then deposited through the pipette directly into the mare's uterus. At this point the pipette is withdrawn.

Some veterinarians choose to elevate the mare's cervix with their finger for a moment or two before withdrawing their arm with the thought that the semen will run down hill more deeply into the mare's uterus. Others simply withdraw their finger as they withdraw the pipette. The author prefers to whisper a little optimistic prayer ("The mare, she is pregnant") at this point as well as "Every little bit helps!"

Semen extenders are typically mixed with the semen soon after it is collected from the stallion regardless of whether the mare is to be inseminated with fresh semen or chilled, transported semen. If the semen is to be processed immediately after collection for freezing, it usually will be mixed with a standard semen extender initially, then later spun down in the lab. After centrifugation, the sperm-rich pellet is removed from the supernatant of seminal plasma and extender, and the sperm is then re-suspended in a specialized freezing extender prior to being packaged, cooled down, then frozen in liquid nitrogen. Freezing extenders aside, the typical semen extender used for fresh and transported semen is a skim milk/glucose-based extender first developed and its use pioneered by Dr. Bob Kenney of New Bolton Center at the University of Pennsylvania. It is commonly referred to as Kenney's Extender.

The purpose of the semen extender is to protect and nourish the sperm cells while they are awaiting delivery to the mare's uterus. It protects the live sperm cells from cold shock, and changes in pH and osmolarity. Extender also protects the live sperm from the deleterious effects of remaining in contact with dead and dying sperm cells within the ejaculate and the seminal plasma itself for unnaturally prolonged periods of time. Various antibiotics or combinations of antibiotics are routinely added to the semen extenders as well in an effort to reduce bacterial numbers in the ejaculated semen, and to prevent any further growth of bacteria within the extended semen. Many large breeding operations and veterinarians whose practices have a large percentage of stallion semen work often formulate and produce their own supply of semen extender, but it can be purchased as commercial preparations with or without antibiotics already added.

Conception rates with fertile, fresh semen can be as good, and in some cases better, than hand breeding the same mare and stallion. Certain breed registries, such as for Standardbreds, once only permitted the use of artificial insemination techniques when the mare and the stallion were physically present on the same farm at the same time. As a result, many more farms used fresh semen AI at that time than perhaps they do now, as many more breed registries permit the use of transported fresh, chilled semen. Even so, fresh semen AI is still heavily used by many farms for breeding resident mares both because of safety and convenience issues as well as a means of extending the "sire power" of heavily booked stallions. With the easing of breeding restriction in many breeds in recent years (Quarter Horses, for example) breeding mares artificially with transported fresh, chilled semen has become increasingly commonplace. Many mare owners today are choosing this option which allows their mares to be bred to distant stallions without the mare having to leave home. Quite a few mare owners opt to send their mares to local "breeding centers" for management in those instances where the intensity of mare monitoring required to breed successfully with shipped semen is not available at home. Conception rates when breeding with transported semen can be just as good as AI with fresh semen, provided the mare and stallion are both fertile and the breeding management and semen handling on both ends are correct.

Means of transporting semen today are widely available. There are a number of commercial shipping companies that ship packaged containers of extended, chilled semen safely and reliably overnight. Many commercial airline companies also offer same day, counter-to-counter service. This option is particularly convenient if the stallion's and mare's farms are within reasonable driving distances of airports. This same day air option particularly helps in those situations in which a mare is being bred to a stallion whose semen longevity is not the greatest and the collected semen needs to make it into the mare's uterus with as little delay as possible.

Various container systems designed to cool and maintain semen at the colder storage temperature (4-6° C) during transport are available commercially. These containers are designed to maintain optimal conditions for semen preservation during transport, but are not truly meant to serve as storage tanks for multiple semen doses for any length of time. With the exception of semen which does not ship well, most equine semen when properly handled and extended will maintain good motility and fertility after storage at 4-6° C for 24 hours, the usual amount of time it takes to collect, ship, and inseminate a dose of semen. However, the fertility of the chilled, extended semen begins to drop after 24 hours; by 48 hours it can drop by as much as 50% on average. Another reason why it is not a good idea to store multiple doses of semen in these containers for prolonged periods is temperatures fluctuate inside the containers once they are opened, even briefly, to remove a semen dose. As a result, the remaining stored semen begins to warm correspondingly, which decreases its overall longevity and fertility.

There are two types of fresh, chilled semen shipment containers available in the United States at this time: disposable and reusable. There is only one reusable system now available, the Equitaner and EquitanerII container systems made by Hamilton-Thorne Research Inc. These durable containers are designed to maintain a set volume of liquid (semen dose{s} and ballast fluid bag) at 4-6° C for 48 to 72 hours, using pre-frozen coolant cans and a second insulated semen holding cup in a large plastic "thermos." Their large, "thermos-like" design resists fluctuations in outside temperatures, making them fairly good at maintaining the necessary internal storage temperatures, provided the containers are properly assembled and maintained by the user. Another potential, additional benefit of this particular system is that the semen holding cups which fit inside the container can be purchased with lead shielding that will protect the semen from irradiation during airport luggage screening with X-rays. The disadvantage of this system is the cost.

Disposable containers have the advantage of convenience, lightness (which may decrease shipping costs somewhat), and reasonable cost. A number of different brands are available that use a similar design. They are made up primarily of a Styrofoam-insulated box with cold packs. Some are designed to carry the semen dose already prepackaged in a sperm-friendly syringe (some types of rubber syringe plungers are potentially spermicidal and should be avoided). The major disadvantage of these systems is that the internal temperature of the package (and therefore the semen) is more susceptible to temperature fluctuations, so the quality of semen shipped during hot or cold weather can be unreliable. These box systems also are not designed to maintain the necessary 4-6° C internal temperature for much beyond

24 to 48 hours, and the semen can start to warm if the package is delayed. Under ideal conditions, however, these disposable systems offer a less expensive alternative for successfully shipping fresh, chilled equine semen.

Proper handling of semen during collection, extension, and packaging, as well as before and during insemination into the mare, is vital to the semen's fertility. Shipped semen is routinely packaged as single dose aliquots, and double bagged in plastic baby bottle liner bags or whirl pack bags. These bags are sealed separately using either rubber bands, heat sealing devices, or incorporated twist ties. Equine semen is very susceptible to cold shock damage, so in addition to being clean and dry, all equipment and extender coming into contact with the raw or recently extended semen should be at body temperature (37° C).

Once extended, the semen is cooled down gradually to reach storage temperature. Light and air affect stored semen adversely. The semen should be handled efficiently and quickly to avoid exposing it to light during packaging. The bag holding the packaged semen should contain little or no air. It is also important to label and identify the semen, and write down the date it was collected and the number of breeding doses contained per semen package (one dose being the preferred number per packaged bag).

It really helps the inseminating veterinarian if the shipped semen is accompanied by a semen evaluation form that describes the pre-shipment parameters of that ejaculate. These parameters include the number of progressively motile sperm cells packaged per dose, the ratio of extender to semen, the extender used, and what if any antibiotics were added to the extender. In this way, the inseminating veterinarian can compare the quality of what was shipped to what was received and contact the stallion manager if any problems are noted with the shipment. Many breeding farms will keep a small portion of each stallion's extended ejaculate to monitor each shipment's longevity, and thus have a backup for comparison if a given shipment has a problem. Carefully assessing and monitoring each ejaculate this way help keep track of a stallion's performance throughout the breeding season.

A breeding dose containing a minimum of 500 million, progressively motile sperm cells at the time of insemination is the accepted minimum number of sperm cells required when using chilled semen to maximize conception rates. It also is an industry standard for shipped semen. There is a gradual (and for some stallions a rapid) loss of viable sperm in extended, chilled semen even over the initial 24 hours post collection. Therefore, the initial packaged dose of extended semen should contain in excess of 500 million, progressively motile cells to ensure that the minimum number of motile sperm cells is present when the dose is inseminated into a mare. In our management system we routinely package a minimum of 1 to 2 billion progressively motile cells in each dose of extended semen whenever the concentration of motile sperm cells within a stallion's ejaculate allows us to do so while still producing a workable semen volume and sperm cell dilution. The volume of extended semen in a typical insemination dose will range between 30 to 120 milliliters (ml), although it is the author's preference not to exceed 60 ml, if at all possible as larger doses can be awkward to handle. Recent work has shown that there is not a detrimental amount of semen backflow through the mare's cervix during insemination until a volume of 120 ml is exceeded. Likewise, as long as the sperm cells are properly diluted with extender there does not appear to be an increased risk of inducing endometritis in susceptible mares when insemination with larger volumes is performed correctly. However, it does not make sense to overload a mare's tract with more fluid than necessary. In this case, more is not necessarily better.

The required dilution rate of extender to semen is typically greater for chilled, transported semen (4-5:1), than for fresh AI (1-2:1). As previously mentioned, prolonged contact with seminal plasma and dead sperm cells is detrimental to the viability of the live sperm cells in the ejaculate. To improve transported semen's survival rate and fertility, extender must be added so that the final diluted concentration of cells is 25-50 million/ml. The final volume of the extended dose is determined largely by the concentration of progressively motile sperm in a given stallion's collected ejaculate. Stallions producing concentrated semen will end up with an overall relatively smaller volume in a dose that provides 1 billion-plus progressively motile sperm cells extended 4-5:1 extender to semen. Stallions producing less concentrated semen will have larger relative breeding dose volumes (all other parameters being the same) as the initial volume of raw semen required to produce the dose will be greater, requiring a larger volume of extender to achieve the proper final dilution. It is the responsibility of the stallion management to evaluate, extend, and package the semen properly to provide at least the minimum number of sperm in the proper dilution for each stallion's ejaculate. It is the mare management's responsibility not only to identify the optimal point in her breeding cycle, but also to handle and inseminate the received semen properly. As the saying goes, "It takes two to tango."

Chilled semen should remain undisturbed in the unopened transport container until insemination time. Once the mare has been prepped, the dose of semen is removed from the container, gently agitated within the packaging to redistribute the sperm cells in suspension, and drawn up into a nonspermicidal, pre-warmed syringe. A drop of semen is quickly placed onto a pre-warmed slide and examined under the microscope to determine whether the sperm cells, though sluggish in the chilled state, are at least motile. A small quantity (approximately 1 ml) is then reserved to be warmed slowly to 37° C (in an incubator, on a warming plate, properly sealed in a water bath, or in a syringe next to someone's skin), and the majority of the semen dose is then immediately inseminated into the mare. The chilled semen placed in the mare is not pre-warmed. The mare's tract is exactly the right temperature and will do a much better job of gently warming the inseminated semen to body temperature. There is always the chance of overheating the sperm and effectively "cooking" it, or of inadvertently contaminating it with water (spermicidal) if a water bath is used. Counterproductive to say the least.

The approximately 1 ml of reserved extended semen is allowed to warm slowly to body temperature over five to 10 minutes. It then is examined under the microscope to post-chill motility and quality. (Is it just twitching or is it zinging about the slide?) The motility of the now warm extended semen should improve over that first observed when the semen was still chilled.

From the standpoint of semen longevity, the goal of breeding with transported, fresh, chilled equine semen is to inseminate the mare within 24 to 48 hours before ovulation. Obviously the closer the mare is inseminated prior to ovulation the better. Ideally the mare managers are able to orchestrate the breeding so that only a single, well-timed insemination is required to accomplish this goal. The cost of repeated semen shipments, unfortunately, can add up quite quickly (there are usually separate charges for each collection as well as the cost of shipping the semen container). From the mare's perspective, her chances of developing post-breeding endometritis increase with multiple breedings during a single estrous period.

Accomplishing the task of exactly timing the mare's insemination requires diligent management. Daily teasing and rectal examinations are frequently required as the mare progresses through her heat so the progression of tract changes and follicular development can be carefully monitored and pending ovulation predicted. In most instances orders for semen delivery must be made in advance, usually by 48 hours before the semen actually needs to arrive on the farm and the mare bred. This requires the veterinarian to predict with good accuracy that a mare will be within 24 to 48 hours of an ovulation two days in advance of the event. Many stallion managers are cooperative and happy to allow mare managers to make adjustments to semen orders within reason in the form of confirmation calls prior to the stallion's actually being collected. Stallion owners appreciate any increases in the accuracy of timing the shipments as proper timing lessens the need for repeated collections of a busy stallion. It is common courtesy and behooves the mare managers to keep the stallion owners informed as the mare comes into and progresses through her heat. Mare managers also need to respect preset collection schedules (frequently collected stallions are on a Monday, Wednesday, Friday, and sometimes Saturday schedule) and ordering deadlines set up by an individual stallion station. Agreeing to breed two horses establishes a working relationship between the parties involved. Stallion managers frequently do everything they can to accommodate the needs of the mares they are breeding (after all, they want the mares to become pregnant just as much as the people on the mare's end). However, it is rude to expect the stallion's owners to compensate repeatedly for poor planning or poor communications. No matter how well managed a mare is, sometimes she will not ovulate as expected, and a second (or even a third) insemination will be required before she finally goes on to ovulate.

As previously discussed, an average, fertile stallion's semen will remain fertile within a mare's tract for at least 48 hours after breeding with fresh semen (live cover or AI). In the author's experience, this is also true using good quality, transported semen (even though the shipped semen is not inseminated into the mare until it is already 12 to 24 hours old). Therefore, except in those cases where an individual stallion's semen longevity is poor, it is not necessary to breed a mare more often than every 48 hours while waiting for ovulation. From the mare's perspective, it is undesirable to breed more often than every 48 hours as the sperm cells incite an inflammatory reaction in the mare's uterus. The resulting post-breeding inflammation is normal, and healthy, young mares will routinely clear the inflammation within 36 hours (older and susceptible mares with uterine clearance problems will take even longer). Breeding more often than every 48 hours increases the likelihood that each additional dose of sperm cells is entering an environment that is hostile due to the presence of inflammatory debris. This harms the subsequent fertility of these exposed spermatozoa. Not only is the mare at an increased risk of developing a persistent endometritis with too frequent, multiple breedings, but the additional breedings themselves provide little added benefit for an overall chance of conception if the sperm are damaged in the process.

The simple rule to follow is first to time the initial breeding as close as possible to ovulation, but if a repeat breeding/insemination is required do not breed a mare more often than every 48 hours. It has become standard practice for two doses of a stallion's semen to be sent within a single shipping container meant for one mare so a second dose is on hand if necessary. A nice idea, but if a mare requires a second insemination, it is far better to order an entirely new, second shipment and breed her with a more recently ejaculated dose of semen than to breed her with the remaining dose from the initial shipment. For starters, the mare's reproductive tract is far more capable of storing and preserving the fertility of the sperm deposited in the first breeding than any extender/container system designed by man. If the sperm in the second remaining dose of stored, transported semen are still motile 48 hours after the first dose was inseminated, then the sperm from the first dose probably are still well maintained in the mare's oviduct. Therefore, nothing is gained by placing additional sperm from the same ejaculate into the mare. Secondly, as we have already discussed, the overall fertility of chilled, extended sperm begins to decline markedly after the first 24 hours of storage. (It is always best to place the transported dose of semen into the mare's tract as soon as possible after its arrival as her tract will take the best care of the sperm.) The sperm in that second, now 72-hour-old dose will not be as good in quality as what is already in the mare. Lastly, the whole reason for breeding the mare a second time, 48 hours after the first insemination, is that she has yet to ovulate and we need to ensure that there will be live, fertile sperm present when she does finally cooperate. Merely placing additional "old sperm" into the mare is pointless. What is needed is a fresh ejaculate so that the additional sperm will be "young and fresh" and ready to go.

The second simple rule, therefore, is to use a completely new, freshly ejaculated and transported dose of semen each time a mare is bred. A second ejaculate obviously is going to add to the cost of the breeding. But not providing a second ejaculate when the mare truly needs it increases the likelihood that all of the costs associated with the mare management and first insemination will be a loss if the mare does not become pregnant. Coordinating a second shipment is also a little tricky as an overnight shipment will need to be collected and sent before the mare is 48 hours past the first insemination. There is always the risk that the mare will ovulate that second night and the shipment will no longer be needed by the time it arrives. In this situation, it is particularly handy to be able to ship semen counter to counter same day air. An order for a second collection and shipment in this situation can be delayed until after the mare has been examined the morning of the second day following breeding, and only ordered once it has been determined that the mare truly needs to be bred again. If she is found to have ovulated, then she is all set. If she still has not ovulated, then the semen can be ordered to arrive that same day and she can be inseminated again.

BREEDING WITH FROZEN SEMEN

Breeding a mare with frozen semen presents an even greater management challenge than breeding her with chilled, transported semen. A wide variation in post-thaw semen fertility exists among stallions. Some stallions' semen freezes well and others not at all. Sperm cells that survive the freezing and thawing processes with reasonable fertilization capabilities intact also do not appear to have the longevity within the mare's tract of viable sperm cells in fresh or chilled semen. Mares bred with frozen semen need to be inseminated within a window of less than 12 hours before but not more than two to six hours after ovulation. This requires very intensive management. Even when management is excellent and frozen semen with at least reasonable fertility is being used, average conception rates per cycle only range from 30% to 60%. In general, it is reasonable to anticipate that it could take two to three cycles to get a mare to settle using frozen semen. Better success rates have also been reported using an increased breeding dose of 800 million progressively motile sperm (PMS) post thaw as opposed to the standard 500 million PMS used for transported semen.

Frozen semen theoretically can be stored indefinitely in liquid nitrogen. The advantage to the stallion owner in this instance is obvious. The stallion's frozen semen is ready and waiting and can be shipped to the mare at the beginning of the breeding season or at the beginning of each estrus period in a liquid nitrogen tank until the moment it is needed. Frozen semen eliminates the need for collecting the stallion and shipping fresh, extended, chilled semen on daily demand. This is especially convenient for managers of stallions that compete, as the stallion's training and showing schedule does not need to be interrupted by breeding.

Collections can be scheduled when the stallion is not otherwise occupied and the collected semen processed and stored until it is needed. Due to seasonal changes in a stallion's libido and semen quality, it is obviously better if the semen collection and subsequent freezing are performed during the physiological breeding season (late spring and early summer). Another advantage of freezing a stallion's semen is that his stored genetic material remains viable and available should the stallion become injured or die. The disadvantage of frozen semen on the stallion's end is the storage and shipment of the semen. Commercial services are available for storage and shipment, but these come at a price. If a stallion's managers elect to store the semen themselves, then it becomes their responsibility to provide the necessary storage and shipment tanks, and to ensure that the liquid nitrogen tanks containing the semen are properly maintained. Stored semen that is accidentally warmed or thawed while in the tanks is irreparably lost.

A container for frozen semen.

Semen is most commonly packaged in 0.5 or 5 ml straws, but also can be packaged in glass ampules or in pelleted form. The actual volume of the final breeding dose depends on the number of sperm cells packaged per straw and the post-thaw motility.

The frozen semen straws are not removed from the tank until the exact moment they are to be thawed for use. Once thawed, the semen needs to be inseminated into the mare without delay. Thawing protocols vary depending on the method used to freeze and package the semen. Some methods call for a "quick thaw" of the semen in a 79° C water bath for seven seconds; others may call for a "slow thaw" at 38° C for about 30 seconds. Thawing instructions for different batches of semen should be followed to the letter. Failure to follow the proper thawing protocol can damage the sperm and affect fertility.

Thawed semen is loaded into a pre-warmed syringe (or specialized breeding gun) and placed in the mare. A small air bolus usually follows the semen as it is pushed through the syringe, through the pipette, and into the mare to make sure as much semen as possible makes it inside and does not remain clinging to the walls of the inseminating pipette. In general, the frozen semen dose is deposited through the mare's cervix to the uterine body in the same manner as fresh or transported semen inseminations, but in extreme cases the semen may be surgically inseminated.

To identify the optimum time for successful insemination with frozen semen, the veterinarian must examine the estrus mare at least every 12 hours once her dominant follicle reaches a diameter of 35 mm. Using that examination schedule, mares are then bred when the veterinarian determines that the mare is likely to ovulate within the next 12 hours. In an effort to ensure that this will be the case, frozen semen mares are frequently treated with hormonal therapies (HCG or Desoralin) to help induce ovulation in a timely fashion. The mare is then re-examined and re-inseminated as needed every 12 hours until ovulation is detected.

A veterinarian does not always have the luxury of inseminating a mare multiple times. Frequently there are only a limited number of frozen breeding doses available. In other instances the mare is the limiting factor. We have already discussed the occurrence of normal uterine inflammation because of exposure to semen. Some mares have an extreme reaction to frozen semen (they will go so far as to pool large quantities of luminal uterine fluid and develop a "sterile" but purulent vulvar discharge post breeding). We believe these extremely reactive mares demonstrate this response largely because of the sperm's concentrated nature as well as the removal of the stallion's seminal plasma from the semen during the freezing process. The sperm cells are recognized as foreign by the mare's immune system and will incite a dramatic immune response in the form of an influx of white cells into the mare's uterine lumen. It has been shown that seminal plasma (produced by the accessory sex glands of the stallion) has a dampening effect on the response of the mare's immune system to the stallion's sperm cells. When seminal plasma is present, the mare's white cell reaction to the inseminated sperm cells is much less than when the seminal plasma is not present. In all likelihood, Mother Nature designed seminal plasma with this quality to provide some protection to the sperm as it passed through the mare's uterus on its way to the oviducts, making it more likely that the sperm would successfully reach their destination. The lack of seminal plasma and the extremely concentrated number of sperm cells within the breeding dose produces these extreme post-breeding reactions in some mares. Mares which have extreme reactions to the frozen semen may benefit from the frozen semen's being diluted with pre-warmed Kenney's Extender post thaw, prior to insemination. For some mares, frozen semen breeding is just simply not an option.

In the author's practice frozen semen mares are palpated and examined with ultrasound every six hours around the clock once they reach a 35 to 40 mm follicle, and the mares are inseminated as soon as ovulation has been identified. The mares tolerate this protocol well, provided extra care is taken to be gentle throughout the course of the many serial examinations. But it is tiring for the humans involved and only really possible due to the "in house" nature of the hospital-based practice. Every six-hour intensive monitoring of the mare does pinpoint when ovulation has occurred within a six-hour window, and therefore eliminates the need for more than one insemination per estrus period.

One final comment about breeding mares with frozen semen. Many infectious viruses readily survive the freezing process and so are readily communicable through the semen. In particular the virus that causes EVA can be so transmitted (infected shedder stallions are thought to be the primary reservoir for this disease). Semen coming from any stallion which is sero positive for EVA is suspect for carrying this virus unless he has been vaccinated and has the documentation to prove he was negative before his first vaccination. A negative semen analysis for the presence of the virus pre-freezing does not eliminate the possibility that the semen in fact contains the virus. Infected semen sometimes tests falsely negative as a result of improper handling of the semen at collection, during transport to the laboratory, or within the laboratory itself. A number of EVA outbreaks have occurred as a result of supposedly negative semen. Stallion owners are typically candid about the status of their positive stallions. But many stallions have not been tested, or frozen semen is marketed by people other than the stallion's owners and the EVA status of the stallion might not be totally clear. Mare owners should carefully investigate the status of the stallion they wish to breed to and if his overall status is questionable or unknown, the mare should be vaccinated for EVA by a veterinarian prior to the start of the breeding season.

POST-BREEDING MANAGEMENT OF THE MARE

Even after a mare has been covered or inseminated successfully, the task of monitoring the status of her uterus and ovaries is not yet complete for that estrus period. It is important to continue to tease the mare and perform rectal examinations daily to confirm that the mare has ovulated and gone out of heat. Examination of the mare's tract within the first 12 to 24 hours post breeding also allows any abnormal accumulations of uterine fluid to be identified quickly and treated as needed. Rapid identification and treatment of mares which do not appear to be effectively clearing post-breeding contamination and inflammation can help prevent persistent endometritis or infection and save a pregnancy. (Such an environment is not conducive to embryo survival when the young embryo reaches the uterus at about six days post-ovulation.) Repeated examination and teasing of the mare post-breeding also aids in the detection of double ovulations when they occur. It is the author's preference to continue following normal mares through the first 48 hours post ovulation to ensure that there are no lingering problems (problem mares are monitored longer). Mares which will receive early progesterone supplementation beginning four to eight days post ovulation are closely monitored. Any sign of post-breeding infection must be detected because infections in a mare's uterus will worsen with progesterone supplementation.

Routine teasing should continue into and throughout the mare's diestrous period. Mares which fail to establish a pregnancy as a result of the breeding activity during the previous estrous period are expected to begin teasing back between 16 to 18 days post ovulation. Open mares (especially those with endometritis) will sometimes return to heat earlier than expected, i.e., they have "short-cycled." That makes it important to keep teasing mares a minimum of two to three times a week for the first two weeks following ovulation. In this way infections can be handled, and estrus in normal mares which have short-cycled for an unexplained reason is not missed along with the opportunity to breed them back.

Examinations for pregnancy using rectal ultrasound should begin 14 days after ovulation. Early embryos can be identified as early as 10 to 12 days post ovulation, but as a matter of practicality most farms begin looking when the embryonic vesicle is larger and more easily identified around day 14. Twin pregnancies identified prior to embryonic fixation around day 16 post ovulation are also easier to manipulate and reduce due to the mobile nature of the embryonic vesicles up until this point. Follow-up pregnancy examinations using rectal ultrasound are recommended between day 18 to 20 and again between day 25 to 30 of gestation. In this way the mare continues to be monitored during early gestation for the presence of twins (surprises do happen), continued normal development of a previously identified embryo, and early embryonic death with retention of a CL or a rapid return to estrus. The subjects of pregnancy diagnosis, early embryonic development, twin pregnancy management, and progesterone supplementation in mares have been discussed more thoroughly in *Understanding the Broodmare*, and the author refers the reader to those sections of that text for a more detailed description of these topics.

CHAPTER 8

Manipulation of the Breeding Season

Left to her own devices, a mare cycles more or less between the months of April and October. Each estrous cycle (or the length of time between ovulations) lasts approximately 21 days, and the mare ovulates 24 to 48 hours before the end of her behavioral estrus period after a variable number of preceding days in heat. Unfortunately, these patterns are not always the most convenient for humans imposing their own schedules on the breeding process. Equine reproductive physiology lends itself to manipulation in a number of ways, and the mare's seasonality, ovulations, and interestrous interval all can be manipulated to suit manmade demands.

Because the mare's gestation length is approximately 11 months, the equine breeding season begins in late spring and ends in early to mid-autumn. Over time, natural selection pressures favored individuals born during the warmer seasons, and, consequently, the genetics of those mares which cycled during May, June, and July in the Northern Hemisphere. However, at some period during man's Western development, January was chosen as the start of our calendar year. Many stud books once recorded a horse's actual day of birth as its official birthday. But for racehorses in particular, this manner of measuring a horse's age started to cause considerable confusion as horses might compete as 3-year-olds one week, then turn around and run as

4-year-olds the next. As a matter of convenience, it was decided that all Standardbreds and Thoroughbreds should have the same designated birthday, and January 1st became the chosen date. It is unfortunate that the decision-makers did not stop to think the matter through a little better.

In order for a mare to foal on or a little bit after January 1, she needs to conceive during the month of February. Left alone, mares are still in late anestrus or spring transition at this time (not the optimal time to be trying to breed a mare!). There are strong incentives for trying to breed mares so that they foal as close to January 1 as possible. A foal born in January will be older and thus more mature than a foal born in June. The older foal will have developmental advantages when the two race against one another as "2- and 3-year-olds" in particular. Older foals generally will be larger when it comes time to sell them as weanlings and yearlings and might command a higher price at the sales.

> ## AT A GLANCE
>
> • Equine reproductive physiology can be manipulated in a number of ways, including hormonally, to suit manmade demands.
>
> • Many breed registries have adopted January 1 as horses' universal birthday.
>
> • Placing a mare "under lights" could trick her system into having ovulatory cycles earlier than under natural conditions.

Other breed registries also adopted a January 1 birthday, so racehorses are not the only horses placed under this kind of winter birthing pressure. Breeds, such as Morgans and Quarter Horses, which have richly rewarded futurity competitions for weanlings and yearlings, also are under the "bigger is better" dilemma. Any time money is involved, there is obviously a strong incentive to meet the requirements, and so it is with breeding mares in what, in effect, is the non-physiological breeding season.

THE USE OF LIGHTS

Increasing day length, or photoperiod, is the signal that initiates the mare's hypothalamic-pituitary axis to resume production of gonadotropins following winter anestrus. In natural conditions, this stimulus begins shortly after the winter solstice (December 21) and culminates in the mare's

A mare under lights.

first ovulation of the breeding season, typically in mid to late March or early April. It is possible to trick the mare's system into believing spring has arrived earlier by placing her under lights to increase the "day length" artificially. Mares exposed daily to an artificial photoperiod of 16 hours will experience their first ovulation 60 to 90 days after the light program starts. The light can be fluorescent or incandescent and must be bright enough so that a book can be read easily anywhere within the mare's stall or enclosure (a 150- to 200-watt bulb is usually sufficient, although mares in paddocks might be under flood lights). The light must bathe the mare in such a way that there are no dark stall corners or low stall doors or fences that allow the mare to place her head in the shadows.

To have a mare up, cycling, and ready to begin breeding between February 15 to March 1, she must be placed under the daily extended photoperiod sometime between November 15 and December 1. It is wise to wait until at least February 15 to begin breeding horses with January 1 birthdays to avoid the possibility of producing a foal in late December. This foal would technically celebrate its first "birthday" when it was only a few days old!

It is a good idea to maintain mares under lights until the natural photoperiod has caught up (i.e., until May). Many farms stable their mares under lights with timers set to turn the lights on at 6 a.m. and off at 10 p.m. Mares can spend the day outside, provided they do not go out until the day is well advanced and are back inside under the lights before sunset.

Other lighting regimens that successfully stimulate mares to begin cycling are "end of the day" and "night interruption" techniques. Studies have shown that extending lighting at the end of the day for two to three hours can stimulate mares to cycle as long as the 60- to 90-day protocol is followed. There is something special about these first few hours after darkness, as this method does not work if the light is provided at the beginning of the day. The "night interruption" technique involves daily exposing the mares to an hour-long period of light, 9½ hours after sunset. It also is not clear why this method works, but apparently this time period is a light sensitive time for the mare and is sufficient to trigger her system. Different farms will choose methods that suit their particular management system best, but traditionally farms have used the 16-hour daylight/day approach.

Increasing day length is the primary stimulus that brings the mare out of anestrus and through spring transition, but diet and ambient temperature also can act, to some degree, as additional modifiers. In colder climates, mares which are protected from temperature extremes might be more responsive to a lights program. The gradual warming of the seasonal environment in the spring probably does play some small role in stimulating the mare's continued progression toward her first ovulation. (A single late March snowstorm, while depressing to the spirit, probably is not enough to delay mares a great deal.) This is not to say that broodmares are best shut up in a barn in the winter. Fresh air and freedom help keep horses healthy, and horses with chronic respiratory allergies might not tolerate being stabled, even in a well-ventilated barn. What it does mean is that if the goal is to try and trick the mare into believing it is spring, then it is probably best that she not spend every day in blizzard conditions. In those areas of the country where the snow doesn't leave until May, the use of a well-lighted and ventilated covered arena for turnout might have an advantage over placing the mare out in stormy weather.

It is also worth mentioning that some managers consider it counterproductive to blanket a mare while she is under lights. However, the light signal travels to the mare's pineal gland via the eye, so blanketing should not have a disruptive effect provided the mare's head is not covered. In the author's opinion, it is always best to keep an open mind. Therefore, if blanketed mares appear to be slow to respond, and are not moving through transition within six to eight weeks as would be expected, then perhaps it might be a good idea to leave off the blankets as long as the mares have an adequate winter coat.

Another somewhat controversial management practice is manipulating an open mare's plane of nutrition in conjunction with a lights program to mimic what she would experience naturally with the change of seasons. During the winter, food is scarce and a horse in the wild gradually would lose condition until the grass returns. In spring, the mare would start to regain weight at the same time she would be breeding. "Flushing" mares, as it is sometimes referred to, involves reducing the plane of nutrition in early fall so that she is mildly underweight (ribs showing somewhat) in November and December. When she is placed under lights, the energy level in her diet is gradually increased so that she is on a slowly rising plane of nutrition. In this manner she gradually begins gaining weight daily as she progresses through her transitional period, and continues to gain throughout the time she is being bred. The goal is to have her back up to her optimal weight after she has established her pregnancy, then decrease her diet just enough so that she is maintaining her optimal condition once pregnant without becoming fat.

Unlike "flushing" in some other domestic species, this method does not necessarily increase the incidence of multiple ovulations per cycle in a mare, but it is thought by some to optimize her fertility and increase her overall chances of conception. This management practice should only be undertaken by experienced horse managers because it is possible to overdo the dieting and make mares too thin. Rapid shifts in a horse's diet can lead to GI upset and colic. When in doubt, it is always best for a mare to get a consistent diet that maintains her optimum body condition (i.e., not too fat and not too thin, but glossy and happy with ribs that can still be felt, but not seen). An additional caveat is that "flushing" probably should not be practiced on older broodmares as it has been shown that aged mares in general seem to perform better reproductively if they are not thin entering the breeding season.

Placing mares under lights is the tried and true method (when performed correctly) of stimulating most mares to enter transition earlier than they normally would under natural lighting conditions. But lights programs do not speed up a mare's normal, six- to eight-week spring transitional period. That is why it takes 60 to 90 days from the start of a lights program for a mare to begin cycling normally. Rather, lights reset the mare's seasonal clock so that she enters transition sooner during the calendar year, and, therefore, ultimately begins cycling normally earlier in the season than she otherwise would. The use of lights is quite common across the industry in those breeds that profit from late winter foaling. However, it does have some associated drawbacks, such as the cost of lighting over such a long period of time, the additional workload associated with caring for confined horses, and the effort required to time the lighting exposure properly. While to some these inconveniences are small and well worth the effort, it is man's nature to try to find better, faster means of accomplishing a goal.

HORMONE THERAPY

A great deal of research has gone into trying to identify ways to manipulate mares hormonally in order to speed them toward earlier ovulations. Work with various GnRH protocols has produced variable results, and in many instances is too labor intensive (hourly injections over 24-hour periods) to have much practical use. Recent studies using dopamine antagonists such as sulpiride and domperidone have shown some promise of rapidly inducing a percentage of mares to enter transition and quickly go on to ovulate, but preliminary results have not been consistent with all mares. These responses have improved and become more consistent with the addition of stabling, consistent grain intake, and lighting to the treatment protocols. (Again, photoperiod appears to be the most consistent and important stimulus required to return the mare to cyclic activity, and the addition of this stimulus seems to improve drug treatment responses in those mares which are going to respond.) These drug protocols are not without some side effects, such as mammary development and early shedding of winter coats along with localized muscle soreness in those protocols requiring multiple daily injections. And they are still somewhat labor intensive without producing 100% effectiveness. However, these treatments do show promise of eventually becoming an additional management tool for mare managers and veterinarians.

BREEDING ON THE SECOND CYCLE

Breeding a mare to conceive on her very first ovulation of the year might not be as successful at establishing a viable pregnancy as waiting and instead breeding on the next cycle. Some researchers have mentioned that the oocyte released by the year's first ovulatory follicle is not the same as oocytes released on subsequent ovulations during the season. For instance, there are differences in shape. This possibly supports the notion that perhaps an embryo resulting from the first ovulation could be more susceptible to early embryonic loss in some way than an embryo resulting from later ovulations.

In addition, the endometrial biopsy samples of anestrus and transitional mares differ in appearance from samples taken from cycling mares. Anestrus mares have little glandular activity, and the endometrial tissues reflect the inactive state of their ovaries, whereas the glands and other endometrial tissues in cycling mares, which are under the influence of the ovarian steroid hormones, reflect that activity and are productive. The uterine environment of a mare which is ovulating for the first time that season possibly might not be as ready to support a developing conceptus as an established cycling mare. More study is required on both counts to make more definitive judgments.

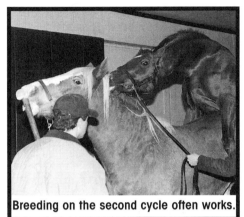

Breeding on the second cycle often works.

From a practical standpoint, it is easier to predict the timing of the season's second ovulation than it frequently is to predict the first. Mares in transition express wide variations in the intensity and duration of their estrus behavior as transitional follicles come and go. Transitional follicles also can become quite large without going on to ovulate, and so it is possible to be fooled and begin breeding a mare to no avail. Once the mare has passed that first ovulation of the year, she will settle into her normal 21-day pattern and thus can be bred with more certainty.

Given these reasons, it is the author's preference to allow the mare's first ovulation to pass and either wait for her to return to estrus on her own or short cycle her back with prostaglandin to breed on the second or an even later heat. The occurrence of the first ovulation can be identified either by the presence of a CL during rectal ultrasound examination or by an elevated blood progesterone level. It is a good idea to monitor transitional mares weekly using either method so that their progress can be monitored and their ovulations identified. In this way management stays on top of these mares and little time is lost getting them bred.

CHAPTER 9

Manipulation of the Estrous Cycle

OVULATION INDUCTION

The ability to induce a mare's ovulation so she will require only a single breeding is extremely useful to managers. It is especially helpful when a mare is being bred either by live cover to a busy stallion or with transported semen. This ability helps to limit the need for repeat breedings and increased exposure to possible uterine contamination. In the world of frozen semen breeding, manipulating a mare so that an ovulation most likely will occur within a 36- to 48-hour time frame also means the mare requires a shorter monitoring period to pinpoint her ovulation. Veterinarians presently have two hormonal therapy protocols available to them, using either human chorionic gonadotropin or Desoralin, to help induce ovulation.

Human chorionic gonadotropin (HCG) has a luteinizing hormone (LH)-like effect and will cause most estrus mares with a viable follicle that is at least 35 mm in diameter to ovulate within 48 hours of treatment. However, an estrus mare's ovaries still must be examined by rectal palpation and/or ultrasound to determine the presence of a follicle that is at least 35 mm in diameter. Many mares tease hot with only a 30mm follicle. Using a blind approach to treat mares with HCG will not yield reliable results, as mares with follicles less than 35mm in diameter frequently will not respond (i.e., they are unlikely to ovulate within 48 hours). When used correctly, however, HCG is fairly but not absolutely reliable in inducing mares to ovulate, and as such is a particularly useful tool in a veterinarian's arsenal when combined with good overall estrus management. Mares which have been monitored accurately so that they are being bred at the optimal point in their cycle can be injected with HCG at the time of breeding with the rela-

> **AT A GLANCE**
>
> • Different hormonal therapies can induce or inhibit ovulation.
>
> • Hormonal therapy can be useful when the objective is to breed a mare only once during her cycle.
>
> • Use of prostaglandin may produce side effects such as sweating, cramps, and colic.
>
> • The use of hormonal therapies must be done in conjunction with good breeding management.

tive assurance that they then will ovulate within 48 hours and not require rebreeding. (The mare still needs to be monitored post-breeding to make sure this is indeed the case.) Some veterinary managers even prefer to give the mare an HCG injection the day before a scheduled trip to the breeding shed or the day before the shipped semen arrives. This management technique assumes that the mare which is bred 12 to 24 hours post HCG injection is within 24 hours of ovulating. This works well unless the mare ovulates sooner than anticipated, if the transported semen is delayed, or if the breeding shed appointment has to be shuffled at the last moment.

In most cases, once a mare with at least a 35 mm follicle has received the HCG, you are committed and there is no turning back the clock. The mare is going to ovulate and all the managers can do is hope the semen is found or she can make it to the stallion in time. On more than one occasion, the author has been managing a mare's breeding and had the semen shipment misplaced en route by the commercial carrier. The author prefers to wait until the semen has arrived and the mare is actually being inseminated to give her HCG, "a bird in the hand" as it were.

The drawback to using HCG is that not every mare treated will ovulate within 48 hours as expected. In addition, HCG is a controlled substance and subject to tight handling regulations. All things considered, though, HCG is a time tested and useful tool and the most economical method available for inducing ovulation.

Desoralin is a GnRH analogue. Treatment with Desoralin stimulates the mare's pituitary to produce her own endogenous LH, which in turn stimulates the estrus mare to ovulate within 36 hours provided she has a follicle that is at least 30 to 35 mm in diameter at the time of treatment. At the time of this writing, Desoralin is newly approved in the United States for use in mares. Practitioners report it to be more reliable than HCG in inducing ovulation, especially if follicular parameters vary somewhat from the ideal (i.e., the mare's follicle is less than 35 mm in diameter at the time of treatment). Desoralin can be more reliable in inducing timely ovulation in mares which must be bred earlier in their heat period than is ideal. As such, it is probably the treatment of choice in these instances.

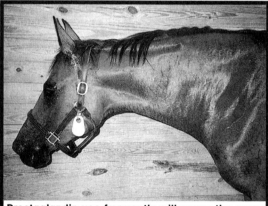

Prostaglandin use frequently will cause the mare to sweat up.

A drawback to using Desoralin is that it is given in the form of a subcutaneous implant and some mares experience localized soreness and inflammation over the implant site. At the time of this writing, Desoralin is also more expensive on a per dose basis than HCG. For this reason, many practitioners prefer to use HCG to induce ovulation in most of their mares and reserve Desoralin for those instances when the timing of a breeding is less than ideal. Other instances where Desoralin might be more effective would include breeding with particularly expensive frozen semen or trying to tighten the coordination for embryo transfer between the ovulations of a donor mare and the potential recipient mares.

ESTROUS SYNCHRONIZATION

Estrous synchronization means manipulating a mare's cycle so that she enters estrus on or around a particular date. This is accomplished by either shortening the diestrus phase with the use of prostaglandin or prolonging it with progesterone. "Short cycling" mares with prostaglandin is most often done to bring a mare into heat as quickly as possible so that she remains open a minimum number of days. Delaying a mare's estrus period by prolonging the diestrus phase with supplementation of exogenous progesterone can be done to synchronize her estrus period with that of another mare or to coordinate her estrus so that it occurs when a stallion is available. It is also possible, using a protocol that gives both exogenous progesterone and estrogen simultaneously, to "program" a mare's estrus so that she comes into heat at a predetermined time and also ovulates predictably from the start of treatment. This "programming" method is particularly useful when more exact timing is required to "schedule" a breeding in advance. An example would include arranging a breeding with a stallion which has an active competition schedule.

Prostaglandin is normally released by the non-pregnant mare's uterine endometrium 14 days post ovulation to end the functional life of the ovarian corpus luteum (CL). Progesterone production ends, and the mare returns to estrus. The mare's CL is susceptible to the "lysing" effects of prostaglandin at any point during diestrus once it has reached functional maturity (i.e., it is susceptible from about five days post ovulation onward). Therefore, it is possible to short cycle a mare with exogenous prostaglandin beginning five to six days post ovulation. There has to be a functional, mature CL present on the ovary for this to work. If the mare is not yet cycling (anestrus or transitional) or is less than five days post ovulation, prostaglandin will not trigger estrus.

How long it takes for a mare with a mature CL to return to estrus after she receives a prostaglandin shot depends on the size of the largest, actively developing follicle present on her ovaries at the time of the injection. Remember, mares continue to develop a new wave of follicles once or twice during diestrus, so the size of a developing follicle varies on any given day during diestrus. If the largest follicle is 25 to 30 mm, then the mare may well be back into behavioral estrus within 48 hours. If the largest growing follicle is only 5 mm, then the mare could take six or more days to return to estrus. Mares which have 40-plus mm follicles when the

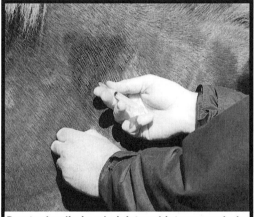

Prostaglandin is administered intramuscularly.

prostaglandin is given can ovulate within 24 to 48 hours without ever having the chance to show behavioral estrus. The bottom line about using prostaglandin is that a veterinarian needs to examine a mare's ovaries rectally before giving the injection to verify a CL and ascertain the status of her follicular activity. The mare then needs to be monitored with daily teasing and examination after prostaglandin treatment to pick up the ensuing estrus and ovulation. In a small percentage of mares, prostaglandin will fail without any discernible reason. These mares could require a second dose 12 to 48 hours after the first. Apparent failure to respond to treatment typically is due to the presence of an immature CL or a rapid ovulation without the mare's having time to return to estrus.

Prostaglandin is administered by a veterinarian intramuscularly, and is available in a couple of different preparations. PGF2a (Lutalyse™) is a naturally occurring form of prostaglandin. Fluprostenol (Equimate™) is a synthetic analogue (other synthetic analogues [cloprostenol] exist but are less commonly used to short cycle mares). Either PGF2a or Fluprostenol can be used to short cycle mares. However, some mares appear more sensitive to the use of PGF2a and experience fewer or less severe side effects from the synthetic analogue. Potential side effects of prostaglandin are usually transient (15 to 60 minutes) and include sweating, crampiness, diarrhea, and mild decreases in rectal temperature. Most mares will sweat within minutes of treatment but otherwise appear comfortable and will continue to eat. A few mares will become quite colicky. It helps to use the lowest possible dosages necessary to induce luteolysis or use synthetic preparations instead of PGF2a, and to hand walk them through the worst of the crampiness.

For a small percentage of mares, it is probably best not to use prostaglandin as it makes them too uncomfortable. It is important to point out that the use of prostaglandins (PGF2a or synthetic analogues) can cause life-threatening bronchoconstriction in mares with respiratory disease. Prostaglandin, therefore, should not be used in any mare which suffers from chronic respiratory allergies (Chronic Obstructive Pulmonary Disease, or "heaves"). Prostaglandin also will readily terminate pregnancy in early gestation mares. So unless the intent is to terminate an unwanted pregnancy, the examiner must be absolutely positive that the mare is open before short cycling her.

One final comment on the use of prostaglandin to short cycle mares. In some instances, mares will begin to show signs of behavioral estrus earlier with a smaller sized follicle post PGF2a, and these heats will last longer than perhaps the mare would normally demonstrate. It is the author's interpretation that premature removal of progesterone will make a mare more responsive to smaller levels of estrogen being produced by the "young," developing ovulatory follicle. The rate of follicular growth is not affected, but because the mare begins teasing in on a smaller follicle, she continues to tease in throughout that follicle's development until it finally ovulates, making the overall behavioral estrus longer. In general, most mares demonstrate fairly typical heats following short cycling with prostaglandin, and conception rates on short-cycled heats are typically the same as for naturally occurring estrous cycles.

Exogenous progesterone — either oral altrenogest, (Regumate™) or injectable progesterone in oil — can be given daily to extend a mare's diestrus period artificially and keep her out of estrus. High progesterone levels generally will suppress final follicular development and prevent ovulation from occurring. In this manner, a number of mares can be "synchronized" somewhat by keeping them all out of heat, then allowing them to come into estrus together at roughly the same time by simultaneously removing the exogenous progesterone. Conversely, the estrus of a single mare can be delayed to synchronize her heat to fit a stallion's busy schedule. (Many mare owners are also familiar with the common use of oral altrenogest to keep performance mares out of estrus for long periods.)

Typical protocols call for a minimum of 10 days daily treatment with exogenous progesterone. After the last progesterone dose on the 10th day, the progesterone is discontinued, and many mares are given prostaglandin to lyse any remaining luteal tissue. For instance, if therapy were arbitrarily begun the day after she ovulated, the mare would still have an active CL present on her ovary 10 days later that would prevent a return to estrus. Just as with prostaglandin therapy, the mare must be examined rectally to ascertain her follicular development when the progesterone is discontinued. Exogenous progesterone will suppress ovulation but not the overall development of subsequent follicular waves. Therefore, the mare could have a variably sized, viable follicle at the end of treatment; thus, her return to estrus also could vary.

A combination of injectable progesterone and estradiol given to a mare for 10 days under a veterinarian's supervision not only will suppress ovulation but also will suppress follicular development during that time. Mares so treated usually will have fairly inactive ovaries follicle-wise after 10 days. Follicular activity will resume and progress at a more predictable rate when progesterone:estradiol (P:E) treatments are discontinued on day 10 and a prostaglandin shot is given. A mare should have a rectal exam at the start of the therapy and again on day 10 before getting prostaglandin. Mares generally will return to estrus within four to five days after the P:E treatments are discontinued, and will ovulate between 19 to 21 days from the start of therapy.

The ovulation date can be tightened up further with the additional use of HCG or Desoralin. The more predictable response of mares to this protocol makes its use highly advantageous in those instances when synchronized timing is crucial, such as with embryo transfer. A number of practitioners also use this method as a means of synchronizing the mare's first ovulation of the season once she reaches the late transitional stage.

The most important point to remember about any of the manipulation protocols is that none of them takes the place of good breeding management. All require careful observation of the mare and diligent teasing and rectal examinations. If the necessary criteria are not followed, none of these protocols will work and frustrated mare managers will still have an open mare staring back at them. Mares are not toasters or VCRs. Giving a mare a dose of this or that without checking her, and expecting her to behave in a certain fashion just will not work. I often find that during the course of breeding a mare it is always best to be diligent in your management and work with the mare's natural rhythms as much as possible and only manipulate a mare artificially when really necessary.

CHAPTER 10

Causes of Infertility in Mares

NON-MEDICAL CAUSES OF INFERTILITY IN THE MARE

Mares on the whole are very fertile creatures. Under natural conditions, when food and water are readily available and other environmental stresses are not extreme, healthy, mature mares conceive readily (often on their foal heats) and produce foals with great regularity from year to year. Horses reproduce much better without man's interference, and it is the unrealistic expectations we sometimes place on mares that can make it difficult for them to conceive. The number one reason fertility rates in domestic mares are perceived as being low is poor overall breeding management. This is followed closely by the fact that we are often asking mares to breed outside of their normal physiological breeding season, and in some instances are making futile attempts to breed mares which are still in spring transition. It is also unfair to expect that an old mare past her reproductive prime is going to become pregnant and carry a foal to term as easily as a young mare will. For all of these reasons, the somewhat low average per cycle pregnancy rates (50 to 65%) seen nationwide really cannot be blamed entirely on the mare.

One constant in breeding mares is that they cannot become pregnant, no matter how well they are managed, if fertile semen is not placed into them. The stallion is a critical player in the mare's becoming pregnant. If he fails to produce semen of good quality or if he fails to deposit it into the mare's uterus during coitus, then the mare cannot be held responsible for not becoming pregnant. Likewise, in AI breeding, if humans mishandle the semen at any point in the process, or if a stallion's semen just doesn't ship or freeze well, that isn't the mare's fault either. Careful assessment of the stallion and his semen's performance are important elements

> ## AT A GLANCE
>
> • Poor overall breeding management contributes to low conception rates.
>
> • Stallion fertility can be a factor in a mare's inability to conceive.
>
> • Early embryonic loss occurs in about 20% of pregnancies.
>
> • Endometritis, infections, and old age can contribute to infertility.

to consider when trying to sort out why a mare has failed to become pregnant following a breeding.

One stallion factor sometimes overlooked is the fact that normally fertile stallions can experience periods of infertility, either because an insult to their testicles (heat or injury) has hurt their sperm production, or because of overuse. Overuse problems are more commonly encountered in busy stallions which are live covering all of their mares. Remember, stallions whose semen is collected for AI usually produce more than enough breeding doses in a single ejaculate to breed numerous mares. Consequently, the number of ejaculates they produce a week often does not need to go up as mare demand increases. Sometimes an overuse problem takes the form of ejaculatory failure due to decreased libido that develops as the stallion is asked to breed more frequently. In other instances, the stallion might have plenty of will; but no horse is a machine, and sperm counts begins to decline with too frequent ejaculation. The daily sperm output of each stallion will dictate how many fertile ejaculates he can produce over a week's time. This number will differ somewhat from stallion to stallion, but on average a normally fertile stallion should be able to cover up to 10 mares a week. Covers typically are spread out so that a busy stallion might breed one to three times per day, four to six days a week.

Once individual ejaculate/week thresholds are exceeded, stallions will begin to miss on their mares. In the Thoroughbred industry, late April through early May is typically the busiest time of the season for a stallion. Mares which miss during this time should not always be condemned out of hand. Good stallion managers know their stallions' limits and are careful not to overbook as this is a disservice to the mare owner. Tactful questioning of the stallion's managers when poor-quality transported semen arrives or when an apparently normal, well-managed mare misses is usually well received by responsible horsemen. The stallion's managers are just as anxious to identify any potential problems on their end as are the mare's managers, and it is good communication that helps put foals on the ground.

CONCEPTION FAILURE

With good management and fertile semen, fertilization rates in young, fertile mares have been shown to be about 90%. In subfertile or old mares, the rates are between 80-90%. Properly managed mares almost always conceive. What happens to the embryo's survival after conception is another story. For conception to occur, viable sperm must be present in the mare's oviducts at the same time that a viable oocyte is present. Many stallions produce sperm with good longevity, and those fertile sperm are stored safely in the mare's oviducts for at least 48 hours. Every sperm has its limits, however, and if a mare is bred too early relative to her ovulation, there will not be any viable sperm left to fertilize the ovulated oocyte by the time it reaches the oviduct. On the other hand, if the mare is bred too late after her ovulation, then the oocyte no longer will be fertilizable even though swarms of vibrant sperm have just arrived to do the job. Even if fertilization still occurs, embryos resulting from aged oocytes frequently do not survive long.

In general, mares which are mated (even with fresh semen) 12 or more hours after ovulation fail to establish a viable pregnancy. Remember, the mare still might be teasing in for 24 to 48 hours post ovulation. Even with careful palpation and ultrasound, it is sometimes difficult to determine how many hours have passed since a follicle ovulated if 12 or more hours have elapsed since the mare's last examination. Conception rates and embryo survival are far better in mares which are bred pre-ovulation rather than post-ovulation. For this reason, post-ovulation breeding should be avoided unless ovulation is known to have occurred within the last 12 (and preferably fewer) hours. If frozen semen is being used, then the mare needs to be bred no later than about two to six hours post-ovulation.

EARLY EMBRYONIC LOSS

The death of developing embryos prior to 50 days of gestation is common in all equine pregnancies, and makes a significant contribution to the reproductive failure in infertile and aged mares. On average, up to 20% of all equine pregnancies in young, reproductively normal mares are lost by 50 days of gestation. In subfertile mares, the percentage of failed pregnancies by day 50 is even higher, 70% or more. Most failures in subfertile mares occur before the time when pregnancy can first be diagnosed reliably with ultrasound at days 12 to 14 post ovulation. The reasons for the loss of early embryos in otherwise healthy mares are not well understood. One way this normal attrition is viewed is that nature eliminates genetic errors that might have occurred at some point before or at conception, or during the early cellular divisions of the very young embryo. In subfertile mares, the high rates of embryonic loss are attributed to both embryonic factors and mare factors. Mare factors are generally considered to be those age-related changes or pathologic conditions that lead to poor overall uterine and/or oviductal environments. A poor or even hostile environment is not conducive to normal embryonic survival and development.

POOR UTERINE ENVIRONMENT — ENDOMETRITIS

Simply defined, endometritis is an inflammation of the uterine lining, the endometrium. Pre-existing uterine inflammation can interfere with conception as accumulated inflammatory products and pathogens within the uterine lumen are injurious to normal sperm motility and survival. Abnormally persistent post-breeding uterine inflammation (unresolved at approximately four days post ovulation) can harm the embryo, which is newly arrived in the uterus five to six days post ovulation. There are many different causes of uterine inflammation, including, as the reader no doubt remembers, the presence of semen within the uterine lumen. It becomes necessary at this point to conceptualize the existence of "resistant" and "susceptible" mares. Resistant mares have uterine defense mechanisms that function normally and can deny uterine access to or rapidly eliminate irritants. Normal, healthy mares experience transitory contamination and inflammation post foaling and post breeding, which they can clear in a timely fashion so that there are no adverse effects on their subsequent fertility. Susceptible mares have one or multiple breakdowns in their uterine defense mechanisms, allowing easy contamination of the uterine environment. Once contaminated, these mares cannot readily clear inflammatory debris and invading organisms. Contamination and insults that normally would result only in transitory inflammation in a healthy mare result in a persistent inflammation in a susceptible mare. Susceptible mares easily develop established inflammation and infections within their uterine environments, and even when cleaned up these mares often succumb to recurrent infections with each new insult (i.e., breeding).

The uterine defense mechanisms include good conformation, anatomic barriers to contamination, uterine clearance, and the actions of white blood cells. All of these can be adversely affected by phase of cycle, aging, parity (number of births), injury, and poor condition.

A majority of infertile, susceptible mares have one or more anatomic predispositions toward developing endometritis. Mares with poor perineal conformation — their vulva is sloped and raised above the pelvic floor, and/or whose vulvar lips fail to join together in a tight seal — are predisposed to developing pneumovagina. Poor conformation can exist from the beginning or develop as the mare experiences trauma to these structures, ages, or grows thin. This problem is further compounded in mares which, because of multiple births or injury, no longer have a tight vestibular-vaginal sphincter that could compensate for a somewhat defective vulvar conformation to block incoming air. During estrus, the mare's cervix is open, and the air that slips by the poorly conformed vulva and vestibular-vaginal sphincter has ready access to the uterine lumen. In addition, the tissue-softening effects of estrogen produced by the ovulatory follicle during estrus can cause a mare with seemingly normal perineal conformation and adequate seals during diestrus to windsuck intermittently. Air that gains access to the vagina and uterus often carries fecal debris with it, and is a source of contamination and chronic irritation.

Visual examination of a mare's perineal and vulvar conformations along with careful listening for an intake of air when the vulvar lips are parted are ways of assessing the likelihood of developing pneumovagina. The relative ease of passing a vaginal speculum through a mare's vestibular-vaginal sphincter provides a means of grossly assessing the integrity of this second anatomical barrier. Pneumovagina is confirmed by the finding of pre-existing air distension of the vaginal cavity along with a reddened vaginal mucosa and also sometimes a frothy exudate with or without contaminating debris on speculum examination. The presence of air within the uterus detected during an ultrasound examination of a mare which has not had any recent vaginal manipulation also confirms the occurrence of "windsucking."

The mare's muscular cervix normally forms a tight, impenetrable seal under the influence of progesterone during diestrus. The seal's integrity is vital in protecting a developing pregnancy from bacteria and irritants that might breach the cervix and gain access to the uterine lumen and endanger the pregnancy. Cervical trauma incurred during foaling can cause deficits in the muscular, cervical ring that compromise the cervix's ability to form a tight enough seal. Such deficits often lead to an increased incidence of poor early embryonic survival or to the development of placentitis and subsequent abortion of a fetus farther down the road. The integrity of a mare's cervical seal is best assessed with direct digital palpation of the cervix while she is in diestrus.

An example of poor vulvar conformation.

Foaling injuries to and changes in vaginal conformation also anatomically predispose the mare's uterus to contamination. Rectovaginal fistulas are formed as a result of a foal's malpositioned or snagged hoof pushing up through the vaginal wall and into the mare's rectum during birth. The resulting hole typically will not reseal completely as it heals without surgical intervention, and is the source of chronic fecal contamination in the vaginal lumen. The communicating hole between vagina and rectum and the presence of contaminating fecal debris in the vagina can be identified during a vaginal speculum examination, but some "R-V Fistula" may be quite small and far back, requiring direct vaginal or rectal palpation for diagnosis.

Normally, the mare's vagina slopes upwards at a 10-degree angle from the vestibular-vaginal junction to the cervix. If the vagina instead slopes downhill to the cervix, the mare may begin to pool urine in her cranial vagina. During urination, urine normally exits from the urethral opening behind the vestibular vaginal junction and on out the vestibule and vulvar lips. When a mare's vagina slopes down to the cervix, this places the urethral orifice at the top of that slope and some of the voided urine ends up running forward into the mare's vagina to pool at the cervical os. This pool of urine then chronically bathes the cervix, causing inflammation. The inflamed cervix is less capable of forming a tight seal, and urine and bacteria are more likely to reach the uterine lumen during diestrus as well as during estrus when the cervix is normally relaxed and open. (It should also be remembered that urine is damaging to spermatozoa.) As with pneumovagina, some mares might pool urine only intermittently during estrus when the vaginal tissues are more relaxed and the weight of the edema-filled uterus pulls the vagina forward and downward. Likewise, some mares experience transient urine pooling post-foaling that resolves as the uterus involutes and the vaginal and perineal tissues tighten up. Urine pooling can be diagnosed during a vaginal speculum examination, or histologic evidence of its occurrence may be detected upon examination of uterine cytologic and endometrial biopsy samples.

Gravity is no woman's friend, however, and as mares age and have multiple foals the supportive tissues generally become lax and the weight of the uterus tends to pull everything forward. This predisposes mares to chronic pneumovagina and urine pooling. This sagging and dropping forward of the mare's reproductive tract not only increases the likelihood of uterine contamination and inflammation, but compromises the uterus' ability to clear itself of contaminating materials and accumulated fluid.

It is fairly well accepted at this time that delayed uterine clearance plays a major role in a mare's susceptibility to chronic and repeated bouts of endometritis and subsequently decreased overall fertility. Transient post-breeding uterine inflammation is a normal reaction to the presence of semen, and normal mares can clear the fluid, dead sperm, inflammatory debris, and bacterial contamination from their uterus within 24 to 36 hours of natural cover or AI. Contractions of the myometrium (the muscular layer of the uterus) clear the uterus by expelling accumulated fluid out of the uterine lumen through the open estrus cervix. These contractions also promote uptake and removal of additional fluid and particulate matter via the uterine lymphatic duct network.

Susceptible mares in general have a delayed ability to clear post-breeding endometritis in a timely fashion. A number of factors can lead to delayed uterine clearance. Poor pelvic or overall conformation in which the mare has a flat croup or is built "downhill" from her hindquarters to her front, respectively, impairs fluid expulsion from the uterus, primarily because the flow of fluid runs counter to gravity. Likewise, a mare which has a non-pregnant uterus that is pulled forward over the brim of the pelvis so that it sags into the abdomen or that has uterine horns that sag down from their broad ligament attachments to form a "V," is more prone to accumulating uterine fluid. The presence of sacculated areas in the base of the uterine horns also is frequently associated with abnormal retention of uterine fluid. Decreased myoelectrical activity leads to poor overall uterine contractility and is a large component of delayed uterine clearance. Another problem that contributes to delayed uterine clearance is the failure of the cervix to relax and open during estrus. Failure of the cervix to relax blocks the flow of fluid expulsion. There are a number of mares which simply do not experience good cervical relaxation during estrus, and there are others which have cervices damaged as a result of trauma or chemical insult that have become scarred and fibrotic and cannot relax appropriately. Taken to the extreme, a severely fibrotic cervix will predispose a mare to the development of a pyometra.

Susceptible mares fail to clear normal post-breeding contamination and inflammation within a normal time frame. In instances in which a mare is bred multiple times during a single estrus period, spermatozoa entering the uterus subsequent to the first breeding are adversely affected by the persistent inflammatory environment, compromising a mare's chance of conceiving. The chances of embryo survival are compromised in instances in which the mare conceives but her uterus remains inflamed in the early diestrus period and through the time the six-day-old embryo reaches the uterine lumen. The embryo can perish as a result of exposure to inflammatory products and bacteria, or it can be lost if the inflammation provokes a prostaglandin release by the mare's endometrium and the CL is lysed. The longer contaminating bacterial or fungal organisms remain in the uterine lumen without being expelled, the more likely the organisms are to flourish and overwhelm the mare's cellular defenses and establish an infection. A primary failure of the immune defenses of susceptible mares has yet to be demonstrated. White blood cell function and antibody production in susceptible mares appear to be normal. It appears that a decreased uterine clearance capability is the major contributing factor leading to chronic, repeated uterine infections in susceptible mares. Abnormal accumulations of retained uterine fluid are readily seen on rectal ultrasound examination.

The uterus normally is free of bacteria, and unlike the vestibule and vagina there are no known normal resident microflora residing on the uterine mucosa. Transient contamination of the uterine endometrium occurs during breeding and foaling, but normal resistant mares rapidly eliminate the presence of these organisms before an infection can develop and become established. Susceptible mares, as we have said, fail to clear this normally occurring bacterial contamination on their own, and in many cases become infected even in the absence of breeding or foaling as a result of chronic pneumovagina or other predisposing condition. Bacterial endometritis in mares is diagnosed based on a combination of uterine culture and cytology findings. Mares with bacterial uterine infections sometimes will outwardly display a vaginal discharge. On rectal palpation, the infected uterus frequently will feel somewhat thickened and heavy and on ultrasound there might be edema and echogenic fluid. On vaginal speculum examination, uterine exudate might be visible exiting the cervix and/or pooling in the cranial vagina, and the cervix and vaginal mucosa might appear red instead of a normal, healthy pink. The organisms isolated most commonly from mares with bacterial endometritis are those normally found on the mare's skin surface, in her feces, or in the soil. These include *Streptococcus zooepidemicus* and *Escherichia coli* in particular. *Pseudomonas auerogenosa* and *Klebsiella* are also recovered with some frequency. Some practitioners think that certain strains of these latter two organisms are more than just opportunists; they are primary pathogens in their own right. This could be true, although susceptible mares in general are more likely to turn up with a *Pseudomonas* or *Klebsiella* infection than are normally resistant mares. Therefore, the host susceptibility of a given mare often appears to be a major factor in the establishment of these two organisms.

Yeast (especially *Candida* species) and fungal organisms also can be responsible for causing established, persistent endometritis. Chronic, indiscriminate intrauterine antibiotic use in many cases seems to be a predisposing element in the establishment of uterine yeast or fungal infections in mares. Yeast organisms also can establish themselves in the vestibule and clitoris of mares, so the mare's own tract serves as a ready source of contamination by these organisms during breeding, insemination, or uterine sampling by a veterinarian.

Lastly, endometritis can result from the exposure of the mare's uterus to irritating chemical substances. Urine is one. Sterile saline in and of itself is enough to incite a mild inflammatory response in the uterus of some mares. The variety of substances put into mare's uterus in the quest for a cure for infertility never ceases to surprise me, and the use of strong disinfecting agents and other harsh substances actually can cause additional irreversible damage to the endometrium and should be avoided.

DEGENERATIVE ENDOMETRIAL CHANGES

Cystic formations within the endometrium develop from two separate structures. Glandular cysts arise from the dilation of endometrial glands secondary to endometrial periglandular fibrosis. These cysts are small (less than 10mm in diameter) and are primarily a histologic diagnosis made based on microscopic examination of an endometrial biopsy. Lymphatic endometrial cysts arise from enlarged lymphatic ducts and can become quite large (several centimeters in diameter). These lymphatic cysts may be contained within the uterine wall or bulge into the uterine lumen. The fluid-filled lymphatic cysts are readily identifiable on rectal ultrasound examination of the uterus. If they are extremely large, they might even be identifiable on rectal palpation.

Lymphatic cysts are the "uterine cysts" a veterinarian may diagnose following a gross examination of the mare's tract. The etiology behind the formation of lymphatic cysts is not well understood, but they are quite a common finding in many mares. These cysts tend to appear as the mare increases in parity and age, and could be a "red flag" that the mare is experiencing some deterioration of her uterine clearance capabilities. The direct role the presence of cysts might play in contributing to early embryonic death and infertility is somewhat unclear. Large luminal cysts may impede the migration of the early embryo throughout the mare's uterine lumen, thereby interfering with maternal recognition of pregnancy. Large and/or numerous cysts also might interfere with nutrient exchange to the fixed embryo and in embryonic implantation. However, many embryos continue to develop quite happily nestled among large cysts in the base of a uterine horn. In general, unless the cysts are very large (more than 20 to 30mm in diameter) or extremely numerous, it is the author's opinion that the cysts themselves do not cause a problem. Instead, they are a sign that a mare's tract is undergoing degeneration. Deterioration of the defense mechanisms (in particular uterine clearance) results in an overall decrease in fertility, not the presence of the cysts themselves. The vast majority of mares with one or a few small endometrial lymphatic cysts conceive and carry a foal to term without too much difficulty. The presence of a few small lymphatic cysts within the endometrium is expected with time and wear and tear and are not immediate cause for panic.

Many studies have shown a relationship between an increased severity of endometrial fibrotic changes and decreased foaling rates in affected mares. Pregnancy losses after 28 days of gestation seem to be most highly correlated with the presence of increasing degrees of uterine fibrosis, and a history of repeatedly lost pregnancies between 35 to 80 days of gestation is highly suggestive of this condition. Formation of the diffuse microvillous attachment of the equine placenta has its rudimentary beginnings around day 40 of gestation, and the equine placenta is not firmly established until after 100 days of gestation. Therefore, the developing foal would appear to depend on the nutrition supplied by the endometrial glands in the form of histotroph (uterine milk) during much of its early development. It is believed that periglandular fibrosis somehow compromises the endometrial glands' ability to support a developing pregnancy. Diagnosis is made based on the finding of fibrotic changes on endometrial biopsy, and a biopsy grade is assigned to the mare's sample based largely on the degree of fibrosis and inflammation present on histological examination. The worse the biopsy score the less likely the mare is to conceive and carry a foal successfully to term (more on this later).

The reason behind the development of fibrosis in the endometrium is not entirely clear and probably has many causes. Endometrial damage incurred during repeated episodes or in single, extreme episodes of uterine inflammation likely results in the formation of some of this "scar tissue." Mares with severe endometrial fibrosis appear to be more susceptible to developing bacterial endometritis, so it becomes a sort of a "chicken or the egg" kind of puzzle. The development of uterine fibrosis also might be a wear-and-tear type change that occurs along with parity in the mare. However, the degree of uterine fibrosis also is observed to increase in mares as they age but which have no history of previous breedings or endometritis. Therefore, it might occur normally, in part, as a result of aging.

Fibrotic changes are permanent, and there are presently no known effective means of treatment though many, such as chemical and physical curettage, have been tried. It is feared that many of the methods described as possible treatments actually end up causing more damage. Producing live foals from moderate to severely affected mares is largely a result of excellent management and luck.

THE ROLE OF PROGESTERONE

The production of histotroph by the uterine glands and other endometrial proteins that support the growth and development of the young embryo, such as uteroferrin, are stimulated by progesterone. Some studies suggest that some aged and/or infertile mares might require higher levels of progesterone (above those that are considered to be normal for early pregnancy) early on in gestation (i.e., within the first days following ovulation) in order to establish a successful pregnancy. Remember, much of the embryonic loss that occurs in subfertile mares happens prior to the time a positive pregnancy diagnosis can be made. It has been the author's experience that some infertile mares only become pregnant and successfully deliver foals when they are supplemented with an exogenous source of progesterone beginning approximately four days after ovulation. Further support for the idea that early progesterone supplementation might increase early embryonic growth and survival is the findings of some researchers that increasing amounts of progesterone before 14 days post ovulation (in normal mares) results in a higher production of uteroferrin by the endometrium. Embryos that develop within this kind of "enhanced" uterine environment are often larger at 14 days than would normally be expected. So perhaps the promotion of increased production of endometrial proteins in a subfertile but otherwise noninfected uterine environment may "rescue" an otherwise doomed embryo.

Progesterone suppresses the response of white blood cells to invading bacteria and decreases the uterine clearance of materials from the uterine lumen both by decreasing lymphatic uptake as well as causing the cervix to tighten and close. This is one of the reasons why uterine infections can "take off" during the diestrus phase. Therefore, the risk of giving a mare additional progesterone to enhance her uterine environment as described above is inadvertently causing a pre-existing uterine contamination or infection to "explode." A mare must be free of any signs of possible uterine infection or delayed uterine clearance (uterine fluid or edema) before therapy with exogenous progesterone begins. At present, the only means of supplementing mares is with daily oral altrenogest or daily injections of progesterone in oil. A product is being developed that increases progesterone levels in mares by stimulating their own endogenous production of the hormone. If further studies support its efficacy and safety, it could become available for use in mares before long.

OLDER MARES

I sometimes joke to my students that breeding older mares (especially those in their very late teens and 20s) is sometimes like trying to get a grandmother pregnant! As mares reach 12, their fertility begins to decline with each subsequent birthday. The incidence of early embryonic death increases as mares age. For some mares, more breeding attempts on multiple estrous cycles are sometimes required to establish a viable pregnancy. Compounding this is the fact that some old mares experience a delay in their return to cycling in the spring, resulting in fewer fertile cycles with which to work.

Older mares experience a one-two punch to their fertility in the form of increased incidence of degeneration of their reproductive tract and uterine defense mechanisms along with an increased incidence of primary embryonic abnormalities. Just as the amount of endometrial fibrosis in a mare's tract tends to increase with age, the incidence of lesions within her oviducts also increases with age. The presence of oviductal lesions has particular ramifications for the survival of the developing embryo during the first five to six days as it is the oviductal environment that provides nourishment and support during this stage.

As mares age, the overall tone and resiliency of their reproductive tissues tend to decrease (especially if the mare has had multiple foals). Perineal conformation suffers and the uterus tends to drop somewhat forward into the abdomen. Associated with these changes is an increased tendency for aging mares to "windsuck" and accumulate increased amounts of luminal uterine fluid during estrus.

As mares age, so do their oocytes. Mares, like women, are born with their full lifetime complement of oocytes in their ovaries. Oocytes obtained from older women demonstrate an increased incidence of aneuploidy (abnormal number of chromosomes). It is likely to be the same situation in the aged broodmare. Embryos that result from the fertilization of such abnormal oocytes will be defective. Experiments over the years have shown that embryos recovered from older mares have poorer survival rates when transferred to healthy recipients than do those recovered from young mares. Primary embryonic defects appear to be a major cause of early embryonic loss in older mares. The tendency for poor embryonic quality, combined with an aged uterine environment that is also less than optimal, results in overall decreased foaling rates for this class of mares.

CHAPTER 11

Managing Infertility

BREEDING SOUNDNESS EXAMINATION

The first step in managing a "subfertile or infertile" mare is to identify the cause(s) for her apparent decreased ability to reproduce successfully. The standard complete Breeding Soundness Examination (BSE) includes a complete review of the mare's health and reproductive history, a general physical examination, assessment of the mare's perineal conformation, rectal palpation and ultrasound of her reproductive organs, vaginal speculum examination, manual vaginal and cervical examination, samples taken for uterine cytology and culture, and an endometrial biopsy. Ancillary procedures such as blood profiles or hormonal levels, karyotyping, and/or direct endoscopic examination of the uterine lumen also may be performed if results from the basic BSE indicate a need for additional information.

A thorough reproductive history is perhaps the most important aspect of the entire examination and should never be overlooked. Factors such as the intensity and appropriateness of previous mare breeding management, the fertility of stallions bred to, whether breedings were with fresh, transported, or frozen semen, and how many cycle attempts have been made to get the mare pregnant are all important clues as to whether a mare's apparent infertility is likely to be entirely her fault. Many mares are dubbed infertile simply because they have failed to become pregnant on a single attempt, and that is not really fair. Remember that the average per cycle conception rate is somewhere in the neighborhood of 60%, and a single failure could just mean she was merely part of the unlucky 40%. Unsuccessful mares which have been bred only in February or early March could merely be victims of the season. Remember, a mare exposed to a stallion in the 11 months before the examination could be preg-

> ## AT A GLANCE
>
> • All subfertile or infertile mares should have a BSE before the start of the breeding season.
>
> • It is important to make sure the mare isn't pregnant before performing invasive procedures.
>
> • The first step in treating endometritis is to correct any anatomic predispositions.
>
> • Many susceptible mares benefit from post-breeding uterine lavage and oxytocen therapy.

nant. A fair percentage of mares presented to veterinarians for breeding soundness examinations are, in fact, pregnant! This condition, then, must be ruled out fairly early during the course of the examination before invasive uterine sampling (which would likely terminate a pre-existing pregnancy) is performed.

Once the gross anatomy and condition of the perineum vulva, vestibule, vestibular-vaginal sphincter, vagina, cervix, uterus, and ovaries have been thoroughly checked, then conditions such as pneumovagina, urine pooling, abnormal uterine fluid accumulations, and abnormally enlarged ovaries can be assessed. A determination of whether the mare is cycling and, if so, the status of her cycle (i.e., estrus, or diestrus) also is made and compared to the season. The overall consistency between ovarian structures and uterine and cervical findings (tone, fluid accumulations, presence of edema) also is evaluated. Just as important, her present pregnancy status is identified.

Once the mare is determined to be open, the veterinarian then begins directly sampling the uterus (cytology, culture, and biopsy) so that the mare is next examined on a cellular level. In this way, a determination is made of the state of her endometrium relative to the existence of infection, inflammation, and degeneration. The sampling of a mare's uterus in the form of a uterine culture is very common practice in the breeding world, and not only just a part of a full breeding soundness examination. Many stallion owners routinely require the mare owner to verify that the mare's uterus is free of infection before she is bred. This is particularly true of live cover breedings. It is very important to realize, however, that in order to reach the lumen of the mare's uterus, the culture swab first must be passed through the non-sterile en-

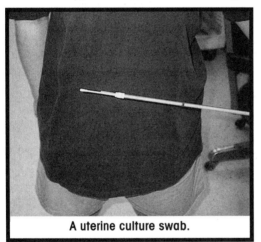

A uterine culture swab.

vironments of the vestibule, vagina, and cranial cervix. Thorough cleansing of the mare's perineum prior to sampling, the use of guarded culture swabs, and careful sampling technique are all employed in an effort to avoid incidental contamination of the sample with organisms not originating from the mare's uterus. Even with the most conscientious sampling techniques, however, contaminants sometimes make it onto the swab and are cultured in the laboratory just the same. These contaminants are most likely to be the very same sorts of organisms commonly found in mares with uterine infections (i.e., organisms that are commonly present on or in the mare's skin or feces). One way to determine whether the organism in the petri dish truly came from the uterus is the purity of the growth and the number of colonies present. One or a few colonies of a mixed assortment of organisms are unlikely to represent anything more than contamination (although the author becomes concerned any time *pseudomonas, klebsiella,* yeast, or a Beta hemolytic *streptococcus* are present). A heavy, pure growth of a single organism is likely to represent the source of the uterine infection in the mare which was sampled. The best way to determine whether a mare is truly infected and the culture results are believable, however, is to retrieve a uterine sample for cytology at the same time the uterus is sampled for a culture. These samples can be obtained using the same swab technique employed to obtain the culture (the swab for the cytology is pre-moistened with some sterile saline), or by flushing a small volume of sterile saline into the uterus using a sterile pipette, then aspirating it back out with a syringe. There are even some commercially available uterine swabs that also are designed to gather a sample for cytological examination simultaneously. With the rare exception of the occasional mare with a very recently established yeast infection, the presence of an infecting organism will incite an inflammatory response in the endometrium.

The presence of the white blood cells rushing in to defend the integrity of the uterine environment is readily observable on slides made from the cytological samples. The presence of more than one neutrophil (a type of white blood cell) per five, high power (40X) microscopic fields on a slide is proof positive that there is inflammation within the uterine lumen, and the corresponding growth of an organism obtained on culture should be considered a truly positive culture. Except during the first 24 to 36 hours post breeding, neutrophils are relatively absent from the normal mare's uterus. Without the cytological evidence, it is difficult to confirm that a mare truly has endometritis, and a cytology should be performed routinely any time a mare's uterus is cultured; otherwise, the culture results are meaningless. An additional advantage of examining uterine cytologies is that it is possible to find evidence of other reproductive tract problems (pneumovagina and urine pooling) based on cells or debris found in the sample. The presence of bacteria, yeast, and fungal organisms also can be readily apparent upon viewing the cytology, and it is possible to get at least some idea of the likely causative organism and some indication of how to initiate treatment while waiting for positive culture results and antibiotic sensitivity testing.

One final comment about culturing a mare's uterus. There is some difference of opinion as to whether it is better to culture a mare's uterus when she is in diestrus or in estrus. It is certainly easier to obtain a sample through the open cervix of an estrus mare than it is through the closed cervix of a diestrus mare, but sampling a diestrus mare actually is not that difficult. During estrus, the mare's uterine defenses are at their optimal and so it is thought by many that any organism present within the uterus at that time truly represents an infecting organism. The exception, of course, is during the foal heat when mares are normally contaminated but not necessarily infected with a number of organisms immediately post foaling. The other thought behind sampling a mare when she is in estrus is that she is better able to clear any uterine contamination that might occur during sampling and so runs a lower risk of inadvertent iatrogenic infection at that time. In the author's experience, careful sampling is successful at identifying true uterine infection irrespective of the mare's phase of cycle, provided a cytology is performed at the same time. My preference is to sample a mare during early estrus as there is also the added advantage of being able to treat any identified infection more effectively while the mare is actually in estrus. If I am performing a BSE on a mare which is in diestrus, I usually will give the mare a dose of prostaglandin at the completion of my examination to short cycle her back into estrus immediately following the examination. That way, she is better able to deal with any bacterial contamination of her uterus that might have occurred during the examination.

The routine BSE is completed by performing an endometrial biopsy using a long, sterile "alligator-jawed" biopsy forceps.

The biopsy instrument is introduced through the mare's cervix manually just the same as the uterine culture and cytology swabs. Once the forceps are placed within the uterine body, the veterinarian then withdraws his or her arm from the mare's vagina and places it in the rectum. The forceps in the uterus then are palpated rectally and positioned at the base of one uterine horn or at any other point in the uterus that has been deemed suspect, and a small piece of the endometrium is retrieved. As long as the forceps are manipulated gently so they do not bang around in the mare's cervix, the endometrial biopsy procedure is painless and well tolerated by most mares. The retrieved piece of endometrium (usually a piece approximately 0.5 to 1cm long) is typically placed into a fixative solution (Bouin's or formalin) and sent to the lab for histological examination. A

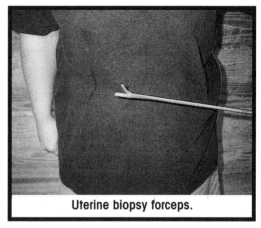

Uterine biopsy forceps.

sample of the endometrium occasionally is submitted for "deep" culture of a mare's uterus as well. Examining the endometrium histologically is done primarily to obtain an overall picture of the degree of acute and (in particular) chronic inflammation and degeneration (fibrosis, dilated lymphatics, endometrial gland atrophy). When considered in context with the mare's history and examination findings, the endometrial biopsy represents the most objective means available at this time to assess a mare's potential reproductive capabilities. Even though the size of the tissue sample is small compared with the overall surface area of the uterine lumen, studies have demonstrated that lesions in the uterus tend to be uniform and "evenly distributed" throughout. Therefore, the findings in a single biopsy sample are usually representative of the uterine lining as a whole. (Sometimes a practitioner may take multiple samples from different points within the mare's uterus if there is any question that one area might be more problematic than another, perhaps as a result of a past localized uterine injury.)

A prognostic scoring system is used by the veterinary pathologist examining the endometrial samples to describe the cumulative changes present. Named the Kenney-Doig system after the men who developed it, this system rates and correlates the mare's endometrial findings with her ability to conceive and carry a foal to term, provided she is well managed. (Please refer to the table.) Endometrial biopsies from cycling mares are more revealing and more accurately assessed than those from anestrous mares. Endometrial biopsies from anestrus mares are normally inactive and somewhat "atrophied" in appearance. For this reason, it is best to biopsy a mare during the physiological breeding season as that is the time when many changes and pathologies reveal themselves.

Kenney-Doig Equine Endometrial Biopsy Grading System:

Biopsy Category	Endometrial Changes	% Chance of Mare Carrying a Foal to Term
I	Normal or only slight changes	80 - 90%
II a	Mild changes (fibrosis, inflammation, Lymphatic lacunai, endometrial atrophy)	50 - 80%
II b	Moderate changes	10 - 50%
III	Severe changes	<10%

(No mare is ever labeled as having a zero percent chance of foaling (unless she has had an ovario-hysterectomy). Occasionally even a grade III mare manages to beat the odds and produce a foal, although the chances of her making it all the way to term are very small.)

Taken together, the role of a complete Breeding Soundness Examination is to identify any problems in a mare's reproductive system and to make a judgment call about her future reproductive capabilities, provided any identified problems can be fixed and she is properly managed during future breeding attempts. As previously stated, many mares undergo a BSE because they have demonstrated an inability to get in foal. Other instances when a BSE might be indicated are as part of a broodmare pre-purchase examination, post abortion or multiple embryonic resorptions, or before corrective reproductive surgery. In the latter case, a pre-surgical endometrial biopsy is recommended because if a mare already has a grade III uterus, it could be somewhat pointless (unless the mare is an extremely valuable producer) to spend a lot of money and put the mare through the stress of a surgical procedure that might have negligible results because her uterine environment is pretty much shot. In instances when a BSE is performed primarily as an infertility work up, it is best to perform the examination as far in advance of the next breeding season as possible This way there is plenty of time to correct any correctable problems and less time will be lost during the next season. Barren mares should have a BSE performed during the late summer or early fall. This is well in advance of the next season and the mare in question likely will still be cycling during this time. Whether a full BSE is performed at the initial work up of a mare depends on the circumstances. A potential buyer of a young maiden mare which presents for a pre-purchase examination with no identifiable physical abnormalities on visual or palpable examination may opt to forgo a uterine cytology, culture, and biopsy. During the breeding season, a well-managed mare which already has a Caslick's and "specs clean" initially might require only a culture/cytology following an unsuccessful breeding attempt. The bottom line, however, is that if a mare has had recurrent problems for no apparent reason, and her management pre and post breeding has been excellent, it is probably time to take a second full look at her and get a uterine biopsy.

TREATMENT OF ENDOMETRITIS

The treatment for endometritis and the subsequent successful handling of susceptible mares have three objectives. The first objective is to correct surgically any anatomic pathology a mare might have that predisposes her to developing uterine infections. The second objective is to clean up any existing uterine infections before rebreeding her. The third objective is to prevent the mare's uterus from becoming re-inflamed and re-infected following any future breeding attempts.

Any defects in the three anatomic barriers (vulva, vestibular-vaginal junction, and cervix) between the outside world and the inside of the uterus need to have their integrity restored in order to eliminate the affected mare's predisposition towards uterine contamination. Many foaling injuries to the cervix often heal well and do not compromise the ability

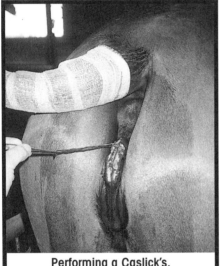

Performing a Caslick's.

of the cervix to form the tight seal so critical during diestrus. The best way to assess the integrity of the cervical seal is by direct manual palpation of the diameter of the internal cervical canal during diestrus. Many times even a complete tear in the vaginal cervical os does not compromise the ability of the cervical body and internal os to close completely. However, in those instances where the cervical lumen remains somewhat dilated due to the presence of a previous tear, it needs to be surgically repaired by an experienced surgeon. It should be remembered that once a mare tears her cervix she is likely to do it again at subsequent foalings even after it has been surgically repaired once (scar tissue has a tendency to re-tear instead of stretching). Mares which have had cervical tears need to have their cervical integrity re-evaluated following each subsequent foaling. Laxity in the vestibular-vaginal sphincter is difficult to address, but reconstructive surgery on the roof of the vestibule to reconstruct the perineal body somewhat could help those mares which continue to windsuck despite having a Caslick's. Far and a way the most common problem found in a majority of subfertile mares is the presence of poor perineal/vulvar conformation. For these mares, a simple Caslick's procedure can turn around fertility literally overnight provided there has not already been too much damage done to the endometrium as a result of the chronic pneumovagina.

A Caslick's is a surgical procedure in which the edges of the vulvar lips are surgically cut and then sewn together starting from the top of the vulva and ending at or just below the level of the pelvic floor. The sewn portion of the vulvar lips heal together to form a protective barrier that prevents the mare from "windsucking." The vulvar lips are not sewn completely together so the mare is still able to urinate freely and discharge can still drain through the vulvar lips. Depending on the diameter of the remaining vulvar opening, the mare might have to have her Caslick's opened and reclosed to permit natural breeding or AI, but in all instances these mares require opening approximately two weeks before foaling so that they do not tear themselves trying to push the foal through.

Vaginal urine pooling, if intermittent, does not always warrant surgical repair. Many mares will urine pool in the immediate period post foaling but spontaneously resolve once the pelvic tissues tighten up and uterine involution returns the uterus to a more normal non-pregnant size. Some mares which only urine pool for a brief time during estrus and are not inflamed can be managed by literally "sopping up" the urine with sterile gauze before breeding or inseminating to dry up the mess in the vagina. Other practitioners use specific acupuncture points that sometimes will cause a mare's perineal and pelvic tissues to tighten up enough to resolve the problem. Mares which chronically pool urine in their vaginas require reconstructive surgery to extend the length of the urethra artificially and effectively place the urethral opening on the downside of the vestibular slope so that the stream of urine can no longer partially backflow into the vagina. This procedure is technically a little tricky and sometimes the tissues forming the artificial urethral extension fail to heal together without the formation of little gaps in the tissue seal. When this occurs, the mare will frequently leak a little urine through these gaps each time she urinates, and this escaping urine again will pool in the cranial vagina. For this reason, it is not uncommon to have to perform a urethral extension procedure more than once before it finally heals correctly.

Recto-vaginal fistulas, likewise, must be surgically repaired to prevent chronic fecal contamination of the vagina. Like urethral extensions, R-V repairs might require more than one attempt before the reconstructed tissues (in this case the reconstructed tissue shelf between the rectum and vagina) heal to form the desired complete barrier seal.

A quick mention of surgical removal or obliteration of endometrial lymphatic cysts is warranted at this point. Remember, the vast majority of so-called endometrial cysts do not have an impact on fertility. But a mare occasionally might have one or two extremely large cysts that perhaps interfere in a direct physical way with embryonic development and survival. These large cysts sometimes can be removed using laser surgery through an endoscope placed in the uterine lumen or by direct manual removal using a surgical snare if the cyst is on a stalk of tissue. Whether removal of such cysts helps is up for debate, depending on whom you consult. Some mares successfully get pregnant following this kind of endometrial cyst removal and others do not. Don't forget that the formation of lymphatic cysts is expected as a mare ages and in many instances is a sign that the mare's uterine clearance mechanism is beginning to work less effectively. Removing the cyst will not cure the uterine clearance problem.

The successful treatment of a mare with an established uterine infection depends on helping the mare help herself by eliminating any accumulated uterine fluid and debris, accurately identifying the offending organism, and subsequently treating that mare with an effective antibiotic or antifungal. The uterine defenses of the mare are heightened during estrus. Uterine drainage is facilitated by an open cervix, and the "seek and destroy" activities of the white blood cells are heightened in the absence of progesterone. It makes sense, then, to short cycle an infected diestrus mare back into estrus so that her own immune system is better able to fight a uterine infection. The author has seen a number of mares which, when caslicksed and short cycled, rapidly cleared uterine infections on their own without need for any additional therapies. When additional means of treatment are required, however, the open cervix of the estrus mare makes the application of intrauterine therapies by the veterinarian that much easier.

Mares with significant accumulations of fluid (inflammatory products, white blood cells, and organisms) will benefit from its removal. Just returning a mare to estrus frequently is enough to help her clear this kind of a mess, but many mares benefit from initial uterine lavage therapy using sterile saline or lactated ringers to flush the debris from their uterine lumen. It also helps to follow lavage therapy with oxytocin treatment, which makes the uterus contract and push out fluid accumulations. Harsh disinfectant solutions such as concentrated iodines and especially chlorhexidine solution (Nolvasan) should be avoided, as they are much too irritating to the mare's endometrium and actually can cause more damage than the infection itself. The exception to this is in the case of some resistant yeast or fungal infections where lavage with a very diluted iodine solution (1% iodine diluted 1:10 with water or sterile saline to form a "weak tea colored" solution) can sometimes help.

Bacterial endometritis frequently is treated successfully with antibiotics, but the occurrence of bacterial antibiotic resistance needs to be addressed. It is a waste of time to use an antibiotic that doesn't work. Shotgun, indiscriminate antibiotic use in mares not only can lead to the use of an ineffective antibiotic but also might cause a contaminating yeast or fungal organism to jump into the mix and take hold. Antibiotic treatment of bacterial endometritis of mares is most effective when it is based on antibiotic sensitivity testing. In addition, not every antibiotic to which a given bacteria is sensitive may be appropriate to place in the uterus of a mare. Many antibiotics or their carrier solutions are irritating to the endometrium. So where a choice exists, only "uterus friendly" drugs should be used for direct intrauterine infusion treatments. It is also possible to treat a mare's uterine infections using systemic (oral, intramuscular, or intravenous administration) antibiotics at the proper dose and frequency. The advantage of intrauterine therapy with antibiotics is the high endometrial tissue levels of the antibiotic obtained by placing the antibiotics directly into the uterine lumen at the site of the infection. Typically a mare will be treated daily throughout her estrus period with uterine antibiotic infusions. Follow-up cultures and cytologies are performed at the beginning of the mare's next heat period (short cycled or naturally occurring) to see whether treatment has been effective and the mare is now clean. If the mare's uterus is still infected, antibiotic sensitivities should be repeated on the cultured organism as its antibiotic sensitivity pattern might have shifted during the previous round of therapy and a different antibiotic might be required.

YEAST AND FUNGAL INFECTIONS

Nothing will ruin a veterinarian's day quite like the discovery that a mare's uterus is infected with a fungal or yeast organism. These types of uterine infections can be extremely difficult to clean up, and it is not unusual to lose an entire breeding season once a mare develops a yeast or fungal infection. There are many different available treatment protocols for dealing with these mycotic infections, which should immediately serve as a red-flag warning that none of them is

100% effective in every mare. In the author's experience, it helps to run sensitivity pattern testing on these organisms as well, as I have found some cultured yeast organisms to be resistant to some of the available antimycotic preparations. Daily uterine lavage while the mare is in heat using dilute iodine solutions is sometimes successful. So is lavaging the estrus mare's uterus daily with dilute vinegar and sterile water or saline solutions. Daily, long-term (21 days in some protocols) intrauterine therapy with Nystatin or Clotrimazole is occasionally successful as well, as is a combination approach using lavage and an antimycotic. In the author's experience, however, some mares with yeast infections fail to clear these organisms no matter what you try until their own immune system finally gets around to joining the fight. There is little to be done but hang in there and be patient.

BREEDING THE SUSCEPTIBLE MARE

Once a mare finally comes clean after a yeast infection, it is extremely important to handle her with the proverbial "kid gloves" so that she does not become re-infected down the road. Her own lower tract could serve as a source of re-infection, so vaginal and uterine manipulations should be kept to an absolute minimum, and of course intrauterine antibiotic therapy should be avoided completely in these kinds of mares unless it is desperately needed. Long-standing yeast infections can do extensive damage to a mare's endometrium, so on the whole it is really best to prevent mycotic infections from occurring rather than to have to treat them.

Once the susceptible mare has been cleaned up and steps taken to prevent "casual" re-infection via pneumovagina and/or urine pooling, the question now becomes how to get her bred without causing re-infection upon the introduction of semen. The hallmark of susceptible mares is that they re-infect easily. Such mares will tolerate very little in the way of repeated intrauterine manipulation, and so not only does the act of breeding pose a threat but so does the possible contamination that could occur during uterine manipulation for sampling and treatment. The best approach to these mares is to work very hard at managing their breeding correctly and to broach their caslicksed vulva only when it is absolutely necessary!

Breeding management of a susceptible mare needs to be highly accurate. The best approach for a mare like this is a Minimum Breeding Contamination technique. The idea is to follow the mare very closely so that ideally she only needs to be bred one time, and that one time happens within 24 hours or less before ovulation. It is best that the mare is already cycling with at least one ovulation under her belt when it is time to begin. In that way, her estrus will be more predictable, and hopefully it will be easier to determine the optimal time to breed her. In general, too, her fertility will be better as May and June approach. It would be ideal not to breed this kind of mare until the normal peak of the physiological breeding season, although this approach needs to be balanced with the fact that starting late leaves fewer cycles with which to work. It is the opinion of many practitioners (including this author's) that the best chance of successfully establishing a pregnancy in a susceptible mare will be on the very first attempt of the season. The rationale behind this thought is that susceptible mares frequently will have chronic inflammation in their uterus as a result of previously repeated or long-term infections. Once she is cleaned up and caslicksed the preceding fall, the still somewhat inflamed, infection-free uterus finally has a chance to quiet down and "rest" over the fall and winter anestrus. If everyone has done his or her job well and luck is smiling on the mare, she will not become re-infected over the course of the winter and early spring before her first breeding of the new season. By the time her first breeding arrives, the chronic inflammation in the endometrium most likely will be as subdued as possible. Once she is bred for the first time, however, and experiences that first post-breeding inflammatory response, everything begins to flare up. Over time, this inflammation becomes cumulative with each successive cycle in which she is bred. Also, her chances of becoming re-infected increase with every cycle bred. For these reasons, the first shot of the season is frequently the best shot for a susceptible mare.

The semen going into a susceptible mare needs to be of the highest quality possible. A stallion which has marginal fertility breeding young fertile mares is not a good selection for a mare like this. Likewise, the use of frozen semen with its overall reduced conception rates compared with fresh or transported semen and its increased tendency to incite uterine inflammation should not be considered an option for breeding a susceptible mare. The only exception to these considerations is if a particular pairing is the only possible pairing for the mare and if she cannot produce a foal with that particular stallion then there is no need to breed her at all. In that kind of situation, there is nothing to lose and it is worth a try as long as everyone is aware that the chances for success are guarded and the risk of re-infecting the mare with nothing to show for it are good.

In those breed registries which permit the registration of foals resulting from artificial insemination, breeding a mare with fresh, antibiotic extended semen (or in some cases where the stallion ships well, transported semen) is the preferred method for breeding a susceptible mare. AI results overall in less contamination of the mare's tract than does natural cover. A sterile pipette and carefully inserted, sterilized gloved hand result in less contamination of the mare's uterus with air and bacteria than does even the cleanest, thrusting stallion penis. Secondly, the actual number of inflammatory-generating sperm cells is far fewer in an inseminating dose (100 to 500 million) of extended semen than it is in the average stallion's ejaculate (5 to 10+ billion). If at all possible then, AI breeding has a better chance of successfully impregnating a susceptible mare while still managing to keep her clean.

The next critical step in managing a susceptible mare so that she becomes pregnant without becoming re-infected or persistently inflamed comes during the post breeding period, especially the first 24 to 48 hours. If all has gone well, the mare has ovulated as you predicted within 24 hours of the breeding. In addition to monitoring the mare for ovulation, it is important to monitor the mare's uterus closely with ultrasound and treat her as needed to ensure that post-breeding inflammation is kept to a minimum and uterine clearance is accomplished in a timely fashion. Susceptible mares tend to accumulate fluid in their uterus (it's the main reason why these mares are "susceptible"). Ultrasound monitoring of normal mares through estrus and post breeding show them to have normal trace accumulations of clear fluid that are less than 1 cm in diameter and which clear rapidly from the uterus without intervention. Susceptible mares tend to have much larger accumulations of clear to cloudy fluid that persists without treatment. The longer seminal by-products (seminal plasma, dead sperm, etc.) remain in the uterus the greater the generated inflammatory response. This inflammatory response peaks within 12 hours of insemination, and begins to rise exponentially after that in response to the presence of accumulated inflammatory by-products in and of themselves. Those sperm that form the group that make it to the oviducts to wait for their chance to fertilize the mare's oocyte reach the safety of the oviduct within two to four hours post breeding. Once within the oviducts, these sperm are safe from being flushed during the act of uterine lavage with sterile saline.

Post-breeding uterine lavage performed within eight to 12 hours of breeding, combined with intramuscular treatments of oxytocin every eight to 24 hours post breeding, has proven extremely beneficial at cleaning up mares post breeding. It is important to remember that the very act of lavaging the mare's uterus runs the risk of contaminating it with bacteria, and so if at all possible it is best only to have to lavage the mare once during the post-breeding period. This first lavage hopefully rinses all the initial contaminants and inflammatory debris out of the uterine lumen and breaks the abnormal inflammatory accumulation cycle in these mares. The use of oxytocin daily as needed one to three times a day, for one to three days following breeding and ovulation to help the uterus clear itself of any remaining fluid is particularly useful. Oxytocin works by increasing the contractility of the uterus. These contractions help push fluid and debris out the open cervix, and then through the uterine lymphatic system once the cervix begins to close down following ovulation. The goal is to have a quiet, fluid free uterus at five to six days post ovulation to welcome the embryo. The author routinely monitors all mares with daily ultrasound for at least the first 48 hours post ovulation and susceptible mares daily up through at least the first four days post ovulation. The question of whether it is appropriate to put post-breeding antibiotic infusions into the uterus is a controversial one.

In mares which are bred AI with antibiotic extended semen there is probably no additional benefit to infusing these mares further. In mares which are live covered it is unclear whether the use of post-breeding antibiotic infusions help prevent a contaminated mare from becoming an infected mare. Many thousands of mares in the Thoroughbred industry in particular are routinely infused in this manner within 24 hours of breeding. The antibiotics used vary with the experience and preference of the veterinarian administering them. The majority of normal mares handle these treatments without any apparent harm. In mares which tend to accumulate fluid post breeding, however, it makes better sense to lavage the mare before administering the antibiotic so that the infused antibiotic is not being merely dumped into a "cesspool" and overwhelmed by all the accumulated fluid and debris. In mares with histories of previous mycotic uterine infections, the routine administration of post breeding uterine infusions with antibiotics, in the author's opinion, is probably best avoided.

EARLY POST-OVULATORY PROGESTERONE SUPPLEMENTATION

As discussed earlier, some infertile mares seem to establish successful pregnancies only when they are supplemented with exogenous progesterone beginning prior to 14 days post ovulation, typically starting as early as four days post ovulation. It is extremely important to stress that individuals chosen as candidates for this form of therapy have to be monitored carefully during the post-breeding period and throughout the supplementation period for signs of inflammation and infection. The use of exogenous progesterone in mares with endometritis is absolutely contraindicated as the additional progesterone will drive the infection, and make an already bad situation a lot worse.

ADVANCED ASSISTED REPRODUCTIVE TECHNOLOGIES

It is beyond the scope of this text to go into a detailed description of the techniques and management involved in successfully performing some of the advanced assisted reproductive technologies that are available commercially. A few appropriate points relative to breeding options for infertile mares are worth mentioning. In discussing these technologies, the two presently available techniques are embryo transfer and gamete intrafallopian transfer or GIFT. Embryo transfer involves the harvesting and transfer of a (usually) seven-day-old embryo from the uterus of one mare (the donor) and placing it into the uterus of a synchronized recipient mare which then will hopefully carry the foal to term. GIFT, simply described, is the process of harvesting an oocyte directly from the ovary of a donor mare, then transferring it to the oviducts of a recipient mare. The recipient mare is then bred with the desired stallion's semen to fertilize the donor's oocyte while it is within the recipient's oviduct. If all works out well, the donor's oocyte is fertilized and the recipient mare carries the resultant foal to term.

The best candidates to be embryo transfer donors are young, healthy mares (better embryo quality and better reproductive tract to support the embryo to the seven-day stage). The older or more infertile the mare, the lower the chances for success with embryo transfer. On average, the success rate on embryo flushes from young mares and then the success rates of establishing a viable pregnancy in a recipient mare are somewhere around 60% and 60%, respectively. The procedures are not technically difficult and can be performed on the farm, but usually mares are brought into clinic settings for management and embryo harvest. Mare owners can nominate their potential

A herd of embryo-transfer weanlings.

donor mares to one of several different recipient programs around the country. These programs make it possible to flush an embryo from the donor mare "at home." Then the embryo can be packaged and sent overnight to a recipient center for transfer. This eliminates the need to provide and synchronize recipient mares at home. In general, a mare owner should anticipate as many as three cycle attempts before an embryo is transferred successfully and a foal results. This can become fairly expensive with the possibility of having several thousand dollars in costs with no pregnancy to show for it. Even so, embryo transfer remains a nice way of obtaining offspring from mares which are in active competition, or increasing the total number of foals produced by a valuable mare over the course of her lifetime. Unfortunately, it is frequently not the answer for obtaining one more foal from an old mare or from a mare who has a uterus that is beyond redemption. Also, registration of embryo transfer foals is not permitted by a number of registries.

The main advantage of GIFT is that it makes it possible for a mare with a terrible uterine environment to produce a foal. For old mares, however, it is still not the answer as you are forced to work with an aged oocyte; the resulting poor embryo viability from these old mares makes success more elusive. Disadvantages include difficulty of harvesting and maturing the oocyte prior to transfer, cost, and the presently limited availability of this technique. At the time of this writing, there are only a limited number of large referral institutions set up to offer this service to mare owners.

SWITCHING STALLIONS

Although there is no concrete evidence at this time to support this theory, it sometimes helps to change stallions if

Sometimes a mare will "catch" with a different stallion.

a mare has failed to establish a pregnancy after several attempts with the same stud. Some things are not meant to be, and some pairings appear just to be incompatible. The stallion has good fertility and settles other mares without any difficulty. The mare management has been first rate, and the mare does not appear to have anything wrong with her and she is not getting infected. It has been the experience of many mare managers and veterinarians that switching stallions at the end of the season after multiple failed attempts to settle a mare with one stallion often results in the mare's becoming pregnant to the new stallion on the first jump. Is there some as yet unknown immune incompatibility between certain individuals? Or is it just breeding luck? Hard to say.

A FEW LAST THOUGHTS ON THE UPS AND DOWNS OF BREEDING MARES

I had the tremendous opportunity when I was a resident to spend some time down in Lexington, Ky., at the Hagyard-Davidson-McGee equine practice. I rode with some of the premier equine reproductive veterinarians in the country, and worked in some of the most beautiful horse country I have ever had the pleasure of seeing. The farms were immaculate and well-managed, and the green pastures with their stone walls and painted wooden fences stretched out as far as the eye could see. Everything seemed to center around the breeding and raising of beautiful horses. Having grown up around Thoroughbreds on the racetrack, I was experiencing a dream come true.

I had the distinct honor and good fortune to spend the majority of my time riding with Dr. Walter Zent, who is without a doubt one of the finest broodmare veterinarians in this or any other country. I learned a great deal from Walter (and continue to do so to this day) as we traveled from farm to farm. On one particular occasion, we were presented with two mares which were in heat and booked to the same stallion. We had been following both these mares through their heats for a couple of days and both mares were about three or four days from the beginning of showing receptivity to the teaser. The stallion was a busy, popular sire and he had only one available appointment for breeding on that particular day, but was wide open for the following day. We examined the first mare, an older mare (late teens if I remember correctly) who had gone barren the previous year, but had produced multiple stakes winners in the past. This would be the second attempt at settling this particular mare. She was teasing red hot and had a palpable 50 mm follicle on one ovary that was tense, but a cervix that was butter soft. The second mare was a famous European stakes winner who had her first foal by her side and was presently teasing red hot on her 30-day heat. (It was mid- to late March by the way.) This second mare also had a palpable 50 mm follicle that was perhaps a little less tense than the first mare's and a soft cervix.

Walter, the farm manager, and I looked at each other. Now what? It was important that both of these mares get in foal. We reached for the ultrasound machine. On ultrasound examination, the size of both mares' follicles were confirmed, but the younger mare still had just a little bit of edema in her uterus and the older mare had none. Walter smiled, looked at me, and said, "What do you think? You have to be able to commit and have big enough shoulders to support your decision." I thought it over for a minute or two and recommended that we breed the older mare that day and wait on the younger mare for the next day. To say I was sweating into my socks a little bit that night is no exaggeration.

By the time we arrived at the farm the next morning, the suspense was just about killing me although I think I managed to play it pretty casual on the outside. We palpated the older mare that I had sent to the breeding shed the afternoon before. The sensation the butterflies in my stomach experienced when my fingers slipped over the depression of that mare's ovulation site and as I simultaneously felt her tense up and her flanks quiver a little bit was pure contentment. We then moved on down the shedrow and Walter palpated the younger mare and then let me take a feel. She still had her follicle, but by now it was very soft. She was scheduled for a cover first thing that morning, and as you have no doubt figured out by now also had a recent ovulation on her ovary by the time we checked her again the morning following her cover. I breathed a big sigh of relief and gave Walter what was in all likelihood a very self-satisfied smile. He chuckled back at me and said, "Enjoy the moment. There will be just as many times when the mares will make you feel and look stupid. So it's best to enjoy the victories as they come!"

I looked off into the morning sun and breathed in the rich spring air and thought to myself, "That's OK. I wouldn't trade this life for anything." As it turned out, only one of the mares (the older mare) conceived on that particular round, but the younger mare went on to catch the next cycle. Most mares breed relatively easily; others make you work for it, while others never settle. But when you see the smile in a person's eyes and feel the warmth of a horse's breath next to your cheek, everything evens out and it's all worth it. Enjoy your mares. Breeding is a lot of work, but all the while it is also a lot of fun.

Abdomen — Area of the body between the chest and the pelvis containing the viscera; also called the belly.

Abortion — Expulsion of a fetus between 50 and 300 days of gestation.

Abortion storm — The loss of multiple fetuses from multiple mares during a narrow time frame on a single farm or geographic area.

Accessory sex glands — The seminal vesicles, prostate, and bulbo urethral glands of the stallion.

Adrenal corticosteroids — Hormones produced by the adrenal cortex (e.g., cortisol), frequently in response to stress.

Aerosol transmission — The spread of an agent from one individual to another via vapor droplets that are exhaled by one animal and inhaled by another.

Altrenogest — Synthetic progesterone (Regu-Mate ™).

Anabolic steroids — Steroids that promote tissue building processes.

Anemic — Blood condition in which the concentration of hemoglobin (and frequently the concentration of red blood cells as well) is below normal levels.

Anthelmintics — Compounds which kill and/or cause the expulsion of intestinal parasites.

Apex — The top.

Artificial insemination — Replacing the normal copulatory act between two animals by manually collecting semen from the stallion, then placing it (usually transvaginally) directly into the mare's uterus.

Ascending infection — An infection that spreads "upward or inward" from one body structure into another (i.e., from the vagina, through the cervix, and into the uterus).

Aseptic — Free of contamination.

Atrophied — Shrunken.

Auscult — Listen to the chest or abdomen, usually with a stethoscope.

Avillous — Lacking villi.

Bacteremia — The presence of live bacteria loose in the blood stream.

Blastocyst — Stage of embryonic development during which the developing embryo is a hollow sphere of cells.

Barren mare — A mare which has failed to establish a viable pregnancy after having been bred during the previous breeding season and is not pregnant.

Breeding season — The natural equine breeding season occurs during the spring and summer when day length is long. In response to increasing day length mares begin to cycle. Mares are referred to as seasonally polyestrus, long day breeders.

Broad ligaments — Sheets of supportive connective tissue that form the reproductive mesentery that suspends the mare's uterus, oviducts, and ovaries from the pelvis.

Broad spectrum antibiotics — An antibiotic or combination of antibiotics that is effective against a number of different types of bacterial organisms.

Caslick's — Procedure in which the edges of the vulvar lips are surgically cut, then sewn together from the top of the vulva to part way down its length so that the vulvar lips will heal together to form a protective barrier between the outside air and contaminants and the interior structures of the mare's reproductive tract. As the vulva is not sewn completely closed, discharge and urine are still free to pass outward. This procedure is indicated in mares whose vulvar and perineal conformation predisposes them to developing pneumovagina, and is a surgical correction of a conformational defect that could contribute to infertility in a mare.

Caudal — Near the tail; posterior.

Cervix — In the mare the cervix is a narrow tubo-muscular structure that connects the vaginal and uterine lumens. It is composed of an external vaginal opening (external os), a straight tubular body, and an internal uterine opening (internal os). During diestrus and especially during pregnancy the cervix is tightly closed to prevent outside contamination and invading organisms from gaining access to the uterine lumen.

Cesarean section — Surgical delivery of a foal across the uterine and abdominal walls.

Chromosome — One of a group of thread-like structures found within the nucleus of a cell that is composed of an individual's genes or DNA.

Clitoris — Female organ homologous with the male's penis, located just within the ventral commissure of the mare's vulva.

Conception — The successful fertilization of the mare's oocyte with a stallion's spermatozoa to form a new individual.

Chorion — The red, velvety appearing placental membrane that directly attaches to the mare's uterus via thousands of interlocking/ interdigitating microvilli in order to facilitate nutrient, waste, and oxygen exchange between the fetal and maternal blood circulations.

Coital Exanthema — Herpes Virus Type III causes genital herpes lesions on the penis or vulva of horses.

Colic — Abdominal pain.

Colitis — Inflammation of the colon, frequently resulting in diarrhea.

Corpus hemorrhagicum — Blood-filled, ovarian structure that forms in the collapsed follicle immediately post ovulation. This structure then goes on to organize and develop into the corpus luteum.

Corpus luteum — Ovarian structure that forms post ovulation from the cells that previously lined the ovulated follicle. The corpus luteum produces progesterone.

Culture — The propagation of microorganisms in a nutrient medium. Also used loosely to describe the act of sampling the mare's uterus in order to culture the gathered specimen to check for microorganisms.

Cushing's Disease — Adrenacortical overactivity resulting in elevated endogenous corticosteroid levels. Caused by overstimulation of the adrenal gland due to a pituitary adenoma.

Cycling — Refers to a mare which is undergoing the normal transitions through the estrous cycle (proestrus-estrus-metestrus-diestrus) and is ovulating in association with her estrus periods.

Decomposition — Organic decay or disintegration.

Devitalized — Dead.

Diestrus — Period of the mare's estrous cycle which is characterized by the presence of a corpus luteum on the ovary, lack of receptivity to the stallion, and production of the hormone progesterone.

Diestrus ovulation — An ovulation which occurs during the mid- to late diestrus period as opposed to during the normal estrus period of the mare's cycle. Because there is an active corpus luteum already present on the ovary that is secreting progesterone at the same time that this unusual ovulation is occurring, the mare remains unreceptive to a teaser. The diestrus ovulation can be a fertile ovulation.

Dorsal — Top; relating close to the spine, or the top surface of an animal's back.

Double ovulation — Two ovulations that occur within the same estrus period.

Dystocia — Difficult delivery of a foal.

Early embryonic loss — Failure of an equine embryo to develop and survive past the first 30-plus days of gestation.

Edema — Swelling of any part of the body due to collection of fluid in the intercellular spaces of the tissues.

Edematous — Full of edema.

Electrolyte — Any substance which, when in solution, dissociates into ions, thus becoming capable of conducting an electric current.

Embryo — An organism in the earliest stage of development.

Embryonic fixation — In the horse the diameter of the equine embryo at about 17 days of gestation begins to exceed the diameter of the uterine lumen. At this point the embryo is no longer free to continue migrating throughout the uterus and becomes "fixed" in its position within the uterine lumen, usually at the base of one of the uterine horns.

Embryonic vesicle — Taken as a whole, the fluid-filled embryonic trophoblast membranes/yolk sack/developing allantois and embryo proper.

Endemic — Relating to any disease prevalent continually in a particular locality.

Endometrial cyst — Usually refers to a lymphatic cyst that forms in the endometrial lining of a mare's uterus.

Endometrium — The mucosal uterine lining.

Endometritis — Inflammation of the lining of the uterus, frequently due to either an infection or a chemical irritant.

Endotoxin — A toxin produced and retained by bacterial cells and released only by destruction or death of the cells.

Enteritis — Inflammation of the intestines.

Equine Viral Arteritis — Viral disease of horses causing respiratory disease, conjunctivitis, abortion, and limb and fascial edema.

Estrus — Period of the estrous cycle during which the mare is receptive to being bred by the stallion, and has an ovulatory follicle(s) present on the ovary that is producing large amounts of estrogen. Also referred to as "heat."

Fertilization — The union of a spermatozoa with an oocyte.

Fetus — The unborn, developing individual. In horses, this term refers to the developing foal from day 40 of gestation until term.

Fibrosis — In regard to the mare's uterus, this term refers to the formation of "scar tissue" within the endometrium.

Flehman — Characteristic, exaggerated lip curling demonstrated by horses (stallions and geldings, especially) typically after sniffing urine or a mare's genitalia, but also might be seen in horses in pain.

Flushing — The process of mildly restricting caloric intake through the fall in open mares, then placing them on an increasing plane of nutrition starting in December. This coincides with placing the mares under artificial lighting to increase the mare's "day length." The addition to the mare's photoperiod stimulates her to begin cycling in advance of the normal physiological breeding season and it is thought manipulating the mare's caloric intake in this manner at the same time could further stimulate her to initiate cycling. The practice of manipulating the seasonal nature of the mare's reproductive patterns is done to meet the demands of the artificially imposed universal "birthdays" of some breed registries.

Foal heat — The first postpartum estrus which typically begins three to 10 days post foaling with the first postpartum ovulation occurring typically seven to 14 days post foaling.

Follicle — Ovarian structure containing an oocyte, fluid filled in its later developmental stages. Mares generally ovulate follicles that are between 35 to 55 mm in diameter. The follicle produces the steroid hormone estrogen and is the dominant ovarian structure during estrus.

Gestation — The period of time between conception and birth.

Gravid — Pregnant.

Heat — Estrus. Period of behavioral receptivity to being bred by a stallion.

Hematoma — A localized mass of blood outside of the blood vessels, usually found in a partly clotted state.

Hemorrhagic — Characterized by bleeding.

Histotroph — "Uterine milk" produced by the endometrial glands, this product is thought to nourish the developing conceptus and fetus, and be vital to pregnancy maintenance at least until the placenta has become fully established.

Histopathology — The pathology of abnormal or diseased tissue; also sometimes used to refer to the microscopic examination of diseased or abnormal tissues.

Hormone — A glandular chemical secretion produced by one organ or part of the body and carried in the bloodstream to a target organ to stimulate or retard its function.

Horsing — A term that refers to a mare demonstrating behavioral signs of estrus.

Hymen — The membranous fold that (when present) partly or completely closes the vaginal orifice in a "virgin" animal.

Hypothalamus — Endocrine gland which directs many of the functions and production of various regulating hormones by the pituitary gland.

Immune compromise — Suppression of the function of the immune system.

Immunoglobulin — A protein molecule functioning as a specific antibody.

Immunoglobulin G (IgG) — The most abundant class of immunoglobulins, they provide immunity to bacteria, viruses, parasites, and fungi that have a blood-borne dissemination.

Implantation — The process by which the rudimentary beginnings of placentation are initiated. In the horse this does not begin to occur until approximately days 35 to 40 of gestation.

Inapparent infection — An infection which displays no outward clinical signs.

Interdigitation — Interlocking of structures by means of finger-like processes.

Interestrus interval — Length of time between heat periods in a mare.

Jaundice — Yellow pigmentation of the skin and/or the sclera and mucous membranes caused by high levels of bilirubin in the blood. Also referred to as icterus.

Karyotype — The number and type of chromosomes found within an individual's cells. Each species and sex have a "signature" number and type of chromosomes within their cells, any deviation from which results in abnormalities of development.

Laminitis — Inflammation of the sensitive lamina of the foot. Causes acute and chronic lameness, and if severe enough can result in separation of the hoof wall from the underlying structures of the foot. In extreme cases the coffin bone can rotate down through the sole of the foot or the entire hoof wall can become detached and the horse's foot "sinks" completely out of its supportive attachments. Also referred to as founder.

Live cover — Refers to the natural mating, whether at pasture or in hand, of a stallion and a mare.

Lumen — The interior space of a tubular structure.

Luteolysis — Destruction of the corpus luteum, terminating its production of progesterone.

Maiden mare — A mare which has never had a foal; also can refer to a mare which has never been bred.

Mammary gland — The glandular tissue that produces milk.

Maternal recognition of pregnancy — Term referring to the point during pregnancy when the embryo signals the mother that it is present, thereby blocking production of prostaglandin by the uterus which would otherwise terminate the pregnancy and return the mare to estrus. In the mare this occurs on approximately day 14 post ovulation.

Medium — Substance used to cultivate the growth of bacteria.

Melanoma — A tumor made up of melanin-pigmented cell; very commonly seen as skin (and sometimes metastatic) tumors in gray horses.

Mesentery — A double layer of peritoneum connective tissue that attaches the various organs and viscera to the body wall and conveys to them their blood vessels and nerves.

Metastasize — Transfer of a disease (tumor cell) from a primary site to a secondary site within the body.

Microcotyledons — Microscopic congregations of attachment between the uterine endometrium and the chorionic villi over the entire endometrial/placental surface area attachment.

Microvilli — Submicroscopic finger-like projections on the surface of the cell membrane which greatly increase the surface area.

Morula — Stage during embryonic development during which the embryo is merely a tight ball of cells surrounded by the glycoprotein zona pellucida.

Mucoid — Resembling mucus.

Multiparous — Having born two or more offspring in separate pregnancies.

Necrosis — Death of tissue.

Negative Energy Balance — When the metabolic demands of the animal for energy are greater than what is provided by its dietary intake.

Neonate — A newborn.

Neutrophil — A type of mature white blood cell whose primary role is to migrate to a site of contamination/infection and engulf and destroy all foreign particulate matter and bacteria.

Oocyte — A cell in the ovary, derived from the primordial germ cells, that becomes the haploid progenitor "female" cell that when fertilized by a male's spermatozoa will go on to form a new individual.

Open mare — Mare which is not pregnant because she was not bred during the previous breeding season.

Ovaries — The paired female gonads contain the oocytes and produce estrogen (ovarian follicle) and progesterone (ovarian corpus luteum).

Oviducts — Site of fertilization; tubular structures that receive and support the ovulated oocyte from the ovary, transport it to the site of fertilization, then nourish the early embryo and transport it to the uterus. Likewise, the oviducts support and transport spermatozoa from the uterus to the site of fertilization.

Ovulation — The rupture of the ovulatory follicle through the ovarian ovulation follicle and the release of the oocyte.

Ovulation fossa — Natural indentation in the surface of the mare's ovary through which all follicles ovulate. The opening to the oviduct of the mare is immediately adjacent to the ovulation fossa which facilitates transport of the newly ovulated oocyte directly into the oviduct.

Palpation — Examination by touch or pressure of the hand over an organ or area of the body, as a diagnostic aid. In mares the reproductive tract is examined by palpating it through the rectal wall.

Papilla — Small nipple-like protrusion.

Parity — A mare's status relative to the number of foals she has produced.

Parturition — The act of giving birth.

Pathogen — Any microorganism or substance capable of causing disease.

Pathology — The study of disease; term also used to refer to the mechanisms and/or results of the development of a disease condition.

Perineal body — The connective and soft tissue layers present between the rectum and the vagina.

Perineum — The area between and immediately surrounding the external genitalia and the anus.

Photoperiod — Length of exposure to light.

Pineal gland — Endocrine gland within the brain which produces melatonin in response to darkness.

Pituitary gland — "The master gland"; endocrine gland found at the base of the brain that is responsible for stimulating and regulating many of the body's endocrine glands.

Placenta — Membranes of fetal origin that provide a point of attachment and exchange of nutrients, oxygen, and waste products between the maternal and fetal bloodstreams in the pregnant uterus. The placenta also functions as an endocrine organ and produces a number of different hormones that help to regulate pregnancy.

Placentitis — Inflammation of the placenta usually due to a fungal or bacterial organism.

Pneumovagina — Air-filled vaginal cavity usually as a direct result of aspiration of air through the vulvar lips in mares which are predisposed to this condition due to poor vulvar and/or perineal conformation.

Postpartum — After birth.

Primary corpus luteum — Corpus luteum that formed from the ovulatory follicle that resulted in the pregnancy.

Progestagens — Hormones produced by the equine placenta which have similar effects as progesterone and which are responsible for maintaining the equine pregnancy after approximately day 120 to 150 of the gestation.

Progesterone — Ovarian steroid produced by the corpus luteum which stimulates changes in the uterus to support and maintain a developing pregnancy; maintains the uterus in a quiescent state, and keeps the cervix tightly closed.

Prostaglandin — Hormone produced by a number of tissues and liberated during a number of pathologic conditions; causes uterine contractions and destruction of a mature corpus luteum.

Pseudopregnancy — False pregnancy; in the mare it is the state in which the corpus luteum of the non-pregnant mare has an unusually long life span.

Pyometra — Rare condition in the mare in which there is a large accumulation of pus in the uterus. Abnormalities in the mare's cervix after trauma or otherwise that do not permit drainage of fluid and debris from the uterine lumen are thought to predispose a mare to this condition.

Recrudescence — A return of a morbid process after a dormant or inactive period.

Rectovaginal fistula — Formation of a communicating opening in the tissues between the rectum and the vagina secondary to trauma during foaling. Chronic fecal contamination of the vagina results in infertility due to resultant vaginitis, cervicitis, and endometritis.

Rhinopneumonitis — A herpesvirus infection with EHV I or IV resulting in upper respiratory symptoms in affected horses. Also used to refer to EHV I in terms of causing equine abortions.

Secondary corpora lutea — Corpora lutea that form on the ovaries of a pregnant mare after day 40 of gestation in response to ECG secretion by the endometrial cups. These secondary corpora lutea serve as back up progesterone production to the primary corpus luteum.

Semen — Stallion's ejaculate composed of sperm cells originating from the testicles and seminal plasma originating from the accessory sex glands.

Seronegative — Term referring to the absence of any detectable antibodies against a disease agent.

Serous — Resembling serum; frequently used to refer to an amber, watery, sticky discharge.

Shedder — Term used to refer to an infected individual who is releasing an infectious agent into the environment.

Short cycle — Term used to describe the premature termination of the diestrus period and the mare's hastened return to estrus.

Spermatozoa — Specialized male, haploid progenitor cell derived from the primordial germ cells and produced in the male's testicles which combines with an oocyte during fertilization to form a new individual.

Subclinical — Denoting the phase of a disease prior to the manifestation of symptoms.

Systemic — Relating to or affecting the entire body.

Tail head — The root of the tail where the tail emerges from the base of the spine.

Tease — Process of exposing a mare to a male to see whether she is receptive to being bred.

Teaser — A male horse (stallion or gelding with good libido) used to stimulate a mare to see if she is receptive to being bred.

Theriogenology — The study of reproduction.

Thirty Day Heat — Term used to refer to the first estrus period following the foal heat which usually occurs approximately 30 days after the mare has foaled.

Titer — The measured level of antibodies in the blood against a given antigen.

Toxemia — A condition caused by the presence in the blood of poisonous products of bacteria formed at a local site of infection.

Transabdominal — Across the abdominal wall.

Transvaginal — Across the vaginal wall; also used to refer to entering the cervix and the uterus by way of the vagina.

Trimester — One-third of the length of gestation.

Tubular tone — Term used to describe the quality of the tone of the pregnant uterus. The uterine horns are quite pronounced on palpation and maintain their tubular shape and orientation as the uterus is gently lifted and manipulated.

Twitch — A restraint device that is applied to a horse's upper lip.

Ultrasound — Process by which sound waves are generated by a crystal and pass into tissues where they are reflected back in different intensities depending upon the density of the reflecting tissue or medium. A transducer receives the reflected sound waves and converts the various intensities into an image that can be used to interpret the structure of the tissues being examined. Ultrasound waves do not pass through air or bone, but readily pass through fluids.

Urine Pooling — Condition in which urine runs forward into the vagina during urination and collects in the floor of the cranial vagina adjacent to and sometimes submerging the cervix. The presence of the urine results in a chronic vaginitis, cervicitis, and endometritis due to the chemical irritation of the urine. Urine pooling can occur secondary to poor, sloping vaginal and pelvic conformations, injury, and/or relaxation and stretching of the vaginal structures during estrus, late pregnancy, and/or post foaling.

Uterine cytology — Examination of the cells and secretions in the uterine lumen for signs of inflammation and infection.

Uterine glands — Glands in the endometrium that produce the histotroph.

Uterine lavage — The act of flushing the uterine lumen with fluid in order to retrieve an embryo or flush out accumulated fluid and inflammatory debris.

Uterus — Muscular and glandular organ of pregnancy; in the mare it is a T-shaped organ made up of two uterine horns (left and right) which form the crossbar of the "T" and a uterine body which forms the base of the "T."

Vaginal speculum — Instrument used to view the interior of the vaginal lumen and the external cervical os.

Venereal — Related to or resulting from sexual intercourse.

Vestibule — Term related to the short tubular cavity between the vulva and the vagina.

Vestibular vaginal junction/sphincter — Soft tissue narrowing that separates the vestibule from the vagina at the level of the back border of the floor of the pelvis. Site where the hymen is found if it is intact. One of the three barriers between the outside environment and the uterine lumen (the other two are the vulvar lips and the cervix).

Vulva — The external female genitalia, the opening to the female urogenital tract bordered by the vulvar lips or labia.

White blood cells — Cells in the blood stream that are part of the body's immunologic defense; neutrophil white blood cells will leave the blood stream and migrate to areas of cellular damage and infection as part of the cellular defense mechanisms.

Winking — Act by which the mare everts and briefly exteriorizes her clitoris so that it is visible. Mares commonly do this after urinating and the behavior is exaggerated and also seen in direct response to stimulation by a teaser when a mare is in estrus.

Zoonotic — Any disease transmissible from animals to humans.

Zygote — The initial, single diploid fertilized cell formed by the union of the oocyte and spermatozoa.

RECOMMENDED READINGS

Lay texts

McDonnell, S. *Understanding Horse Behavior*. Lexington, Ky: The Blood-Horse Publications, Inc., 1999.

Evans, W, Borton, A, Hintz, H, and Van Vleck, D. *The Horse*. 2 ed. San Francisco: W. H. Freeman, 1990.

Schweizer, CM. *Understanding the Broodmare*. Lexington, Ky: The Blood-Horse Publications, Inc., 1998.

Squires, EL. *Understanding the Stallion*. Lexington, Ky: The Blood-Horse Publications, Inc., 1999.

Taylor, J. *Joe Taylor's Complete Guide to Breeding and Raising Racehorses*. Neenah, Wisc: Russell Meerdink Company, Ltd., 1993.

Veterinary texts

Hagyard-Davidson-McGee Associates, P.S.C. Proceedings from the 1998 Bluegrass Equine Reproduction Symposium. Lexington, Ky: Hagyard-Davidson-McGee Associates, P.S.C. 1998.

McKinnon, AO and Voss, JL. *Equine Reproduction*. Philadelphia: Lea & Febiger, 1993.

Robinson, E. *Current Therapy in Equine Medicine*. Vol. 3 & 4. Philadelphia: W.B. Saunders Company. 1992, 1997.

Youngquist, RS. *Current Therapy in Large Animal Theriogenology*. Philadelphia: W.B. Saunders Company, 1997.

Breeding Management sites on the Internet

The Horse:Your Online Guide To Equine Health Care:
http://www.thehorse.com

American Association of Equine Practitioners Client Education
    articles:
http://www.aaep.org/client.htm

The Equine Connection:The National AAEP Locator Service:
http://www.getadvm.com/equcon.html

Reproduction section of the Horseman's Advisor:
http://www.horseadvice.com/articles/reproduction/re-
    promenu.html

The Hay.net's veterinary resources page:
 http://www.haynet.net/vet.html

The Equine Research Centre, Guelph, Ontario, Canada:
http://www.erc.on.ca

Colorado State University's equine reproduction services page:
http://www.cvmbs.colostate.edu/cvmbs/rcsu.html

Compendium of animal care and veterinary resources, includ-
    ing breeding management:
http://www.avma.org/netvet/horses.htm

Cornell University's Equine Research Park that focuses on the
    breeding and reproduction of horses:
http://www.vet.cornell.edu/rand/erp.htm

Picture Credits

CHAPTER 2
Christine M. Schweizer, 19, 21, 24, 28; Anne M. Eberhardt, 22.

CHAPTER 3
Anne M. Eberhardt, 32.

CHAPTER 4
Christine M. Schweizer, 38.

CHAPTER 5
Christine M. Schweizer, 47; Anne M. Eberhardt, 49.

CHAPTER 6
Anne M. Eberhardt, 58, 72; Christine M. Schweizer, 62, 65-71, 74;
Nanette T. Rawlins, 71.

CHAPTER 7
Christine M. Schweizer, 80, 93.

CHAPTER 8
Christine M. Schweizer, 100; Anne M. Eberhardt, 105.

CHAPTER 9
Christine M. Schweizer, 108; Tom Hall, 110.

CHAPTER 10
Christine M. Schweizer, 120.

CHAPTER 11
Christine M. Schweizer, 132, 135; Nanette T. Rawlins, 149; CLiX, 150.

EDITOR — JACQUELINE DUKE
ASSISTANT EDITOR — JUDY L. MARCHMAN
COVER/BOOK DESIGN — SUZANNE C. DEPP
ILLUSTRATIONS — ROBIN PETERSON
COVER PHOTO — JAMIE DONALDSON

About the Author

Christine M. Schweizer, DVM grew up in Elmont, Long Island, N.Y., and spent much of her youth working with Thoroughbred racehorses at Belmont, Aqueduct, and Saratoga racetracks. She received her bachelor's degree in Animal Science from Cornell University and her DVM from the New York State College of Veterinary Medicine at Cornell. After graduating, she spent a year in a mixed

Christine Schweizer, DVM

animal practice at the Cazenovia Animal Hospital in Cazenovia, N.Y., then entered an equine medicine and surgery internship at the Rochester Equine Clinic in Rochester, N.H.

After completing her internship, Dr. Schweizer returned to Cornell University's College of Veterinary Medicine to complete a residency program in Theriogenology (reproductive medicine). She spent part of her residency at Hagyard-Davidson-McGee equine hospital in Lexington, Ky., under Drs. Walter Zent and John Steiner. Dr. Schweizer sat her specialty boards in 1995 and became a Diplomate in the American College of Theriogenologists. She is currently on faculty at The New York State College of Veterinary Medicine, where she is a lecturer and clinician in the small and large animal clinics, and participates in managing the Section of Theriogenology's equine herd and clinical equine breeding services. Outside of the equine breeding season, Dr. Schweizer enjoys riding and working with her own horses and breeding and showing her Boxer dogs. She lives in Ithaca with her husband, Dr. Joseph Wilder, and their two young children.

The Horse Health Care Library